satyajit Ray

satyajit Ray

FROM FRAME TO FRAME

SHOMA A CHATTERJI

Vitasta

Published by
Renu Kaul Verma
Vitasta Publishing Pvt Ltd
2/15, Ansari Road, Daryaganj
New Delhi-110 002
info@vitastapublishing.com

ISBN 978-93-90961-85-6

First Edition 2022

MRP ₹ 495

The Publisher and Author gratefully acknowledge all Open Source pictures available in the worldwide web, Creative Commons, Google sources and Wikimedia used in this work of non-fiction.

Editorial Team: Manjula Lal, Alisha Verma, Manukriti
Pictures by Late Nemai Ghosh and Arindam Saha Sardar
Layout and Cover Design by Somesh Kumar Mishra
Printed by Chaman Enterprises, New Delhi

To

my mentor and guru Chidananda Dasgupta who
taught me not only how to read a film but also
a filmmaker and his works through his
socio-economic backdrop during our long
interactions over the years

and

to my parents, Asoka and Sumita Ganguly,
who brought us up in a culturally
rich environment

CONTENTS

FOREWORD

IT'S A SLAP-DASH world we live in today. We prefer movies that rush around from frame to frame in breathless tension and read books that are page-turners giving us no opportunity to pause, savour and absorb details and the pictures created by the words. Action rules.

Much has been written on Satyajit Ray's cinema: on his method of film making, his choice of subjects and stories, his depiction of characters, especially women. Every aspect of the great master's art and craft has been analysed and laid open for scrutiny by both critics and film-makers themselves. His work continues to inspire, and the odd film that breaks away from the breathless pace of modern popular cinema owes at least one nod to Ray as guru.

Shoma A Chatterji's latest book adds to her considerable contribution to making cinema a more complete experience. Taking a step further into her understanding of Ray's films, this book demands a closer exploration of his work and drives the reader into watching the films discussed yet again—this time with eyes peeled for the nuances that Shoma has caught and laid out for the benefit of the reader.

In the best traditions of literary criticism, Shoma treats Ray's films with the critical gaze of a detective holding a magnifying glass to understand the meaning embedded in the smaller scenes, the most silent relationships. Abstractions find space, like hunger as a running theme and how Ray finds ways to symbolise it in film after film, from *Pather Panchali* to *Goopy Gayen*...Hunger is the expected theme of *Ashani Sanket*, but Shoma's gaze picks up the hunger theme in the other two films where it runs as a tributary to the main storyline, and makes the reader aware of the layering that goes into every cinematic work of art.

In other chapters, she delves into the hidden layers behind conventional relationships. Writing on *Devi*, she steps into forbidden territory, asking questions that might have risen in the stray viewer's mind but were left unarticulated. To quote:

> 'Does the old widower feel sexually attracted to the beautiful young daughter-in-law? If no, then why does he probe into her relationship with her husband, which, according to the traditional conventions he practices so diligently, he is not supposed to? Why does he allow her to press his feet, and be beside him the whole day long till before she is installed as the Goddess? Why does he, under the 'excuse' of deifying his daughter-in-law, stop the very young couple from enjoying a normal conjugal life? These questions were unthinkable during the time setting of the story–1860–and they still are among Hindu fundamentalists who misuse and abuse their own ignorance about their own religion.'

Women, human and goddesses continue to fascinate Shoma.

Her earlier books, especially on cinema, also centered around women, either the women peopling the work of directors or women when handled by a woman director, in this case Aparna Sen. Though her wanderings in the world of cinema have taken her into the work of directors like Aparna Sen and Bimal Roy, Rituparno Ghosh, PC Barua and Mrinal Sen, Ray seems a marked favourite. Armed with her magnifying glass she had looked at objects in Ray's films and their significance and symbolism in an earlier book, *The Woman at the Window–The Material Universe of Ray's Celluloid interpretation of Tagore.* This book takes up from there, giving us fascinating insights that leave us the option of agreeing or disagreeing with the author.

Shoma A Chatterji, I have always believed, belongs to the school of authors who stop, look, see, ponder and share. Her books are a mine for the students of serious cinema who look for insights and a deeper understanding of the genius minds that make enduring works of art that hold a mirror to life lived in the times they portray and will continue to resonate through succeeding generations, far into the future.

—Sathya Saran
Renowned Journalist and Author
Professor, NIFT
Ex-editor, *Femina* and *DNA*

ACKNOWLEDGEMENTS

I WROTE THIS book during the lockdown last year and it helped keep me away from depression. My deep gratitude goes first of all to Renu Kaul Verma of Vitasta Publishing who decided to publish my collection of essays on the cinema of Satyajit Ray, my third book with publishing house. For that, I owe it to her entire editorial team in general and Alisha Verma in particular for her patience, along with Manjula Lal for her very positive suggestions.

This perspective on some unusual features in Ray's films came mainly through watching his films again and again first on the wide screen, then on the small screen and finally, on OTT platforms—which also marks my long journey through the highways and bylanes of Indian cinema in general and Satyajit Ray in particular. Directly and indirectly, my understanding was enhanced by some of the best writers on Ray and the wider community of film scholars.

I must extend my emotional and moral thanks to my husband, Ajoy, for just being there beside me, through storms and silences, fights and solutions, allowing me my space, and for tolerating a workaholic wife like me for more than fifty-six years. He knows how to remain in the background when the wife needs to be out there in front.

Ishaan, our grandson, now all of twenty-one, makes his round-the-clock know-it-all-ness worth the while by leaving behind a vacuum for us to cope with when he goes home to his parents. Much of the relief trigger comes from him.

My late parents, Asoka and Sumita Ganguly, cannot be thanked because parents deserve to be remembered and loved, not thanked. But I can never forget their bringing us up in a culturally rich environment in Bombay soaked in cinema, theatre and literature ranging from Marx to Tagore to New Theatres and Pankaj Mullick. I am more grateful to my mother because of her tremendous courage to work her way through the most difficult times of her life, her creative magic that turned her into a surprise poet much after she was sixty.

They taught us the meaning of being Indian first and then Bengali though we were born and brought up far away from the Bengali language, culture and geography. They shaped the mould into which we just needed to pour ourselves to become good, informed and creative human beings. Whether we poured ourselves into that mould or went out of shape while growing up is for the world out there to decide.

Last, but never the least, I extend a thanks in advance to all my readers who may want to read this book and perhaps find new windows opening up with each essay. That will be the fulfillment of my writing.

PREFACE

AS A FILM journalist, I corresponded with Satyajit Ray between 1964—the first time we exchanged a few letters—and 1984, when I received the last letter from him. We met at film festivals every year but I found it difficult to approach him because he was surrounded by around three rings of chaperones, cutlery, mediapersons and photographers.

I once called him up asking for a one-on-one at his residence but his response was: 'You know me already quite well. We have corresponded. You are also writing about my films. So, what do you need an interview for?' And that was it. He was just too big and I much too small for me to persist.

I first watched *Pather Panchali* when I was around thirteen years at Maratha Mandir in Bombay (now Mumbai) with a young production assistant from RK Studios who wanted to watch this film everyone was talking about and which was winning awards left, right and centre. The theatre was almost empty.

'That Ray is so tall,' is all he was able to say about Ray by way of introduction. He was a nice guy—I do not recall his name—but he went to sleep as soon as the film began and woke up just a few minutes before it ended. 'Boring film *hai bhai, kaise isko itna* award *mila*?' (It's a boring film, how did it get so many awards?) he yawned as we walked out. He escorted me to the bus stop from where I would ride to Shivaji Park as he had promised my mother. I did not understand the film either and wondered why everyone was falling all over it.

My parents were naturally disappointed with my cold response to *Pather Panchali*. They were huge cinebuffs who watched every English film screened at Bombay's Shree Cinema and Chitra Talkies, where Bangla films were screened only on Sunday mornings. Later, Bangla films began to be screened at Lotus Cinema in Worli.

Among the scenes that did touch a deep chord in me was the huge, moving shadow on the wall of the doddering old Indir Thakrun narrating a scary but very familiar fairy tale to the two kids, Apu and Durga. Then there was Sarbajaya's cruel treatment of Indir Thakrun and the old woman's death suggested simply by the rolling of her dented vessel down the rocks and into the pond, sending ripples all around.

I had not read the original novel *Pather Panchali* till then. When my mother remembered this, she brought me an abridged edition for children called *Aam Aantir Bhenpu* with a beautiful cover designed by Ray himself. I practically gulped it down over three or four days, shrugging off Ma's scoldings for habitually avoiding homework.

I watched *Pather Panchali* many times over the years, each time carrying away with me a different reading of the film. I understood one thing about Ray as a filmmaker—he had the rare ability to transcend the limits of literature while turning a novel into a film. His dialogues sounded just like we spoke in our normal lives: nothing decorative, neither pedantic, nor arrogant or even dramatic in any way. And his casting of actors, even known names like Chhabi Biswas and Tulsi Chakraborty, was like a conjuring act.

It was exam time for me when *Aparajito* was released but I watched it later. A scene that became embedded in my teenage mind was a growing Apu trying to explain to his mother the revolution of the earth around the sun with a fruit or two; I felt very very sad when I saw Sarbajaya waiting in vain under a tree, leaning against its trunk, for the son who had assured her that he would be back from the city. We do not see her dying but understand what has happened as the camera focuses on the tree under which she usually waits, as the sound of crickets permeates the air and the flickering of fireflies can be seen. I will never forget this microcosm of the universality of a mother's pain when she realises that her son has left forever.

By the time *Kanchenjunga* (1962) released at Lotus Cinema, I had just joined college and was already a big Ray fan. Why, I could not point out except that his films were so moving that you carried them out of the theatre with you. I watched three shows of the film over two weeks; my parents did not complain probably because they liked the fact that I was developing a taste for good cinema. *Kanchenjunga*, like Kidar Sharma's *Mahal* which I saw many years after it was released, haunted me for weeks together. It was the cinematography and the editing that held me captive though I had no idea about these techniques and their use in cinema. I enjoyed the low-key treatment of the relationships, the slightly Leftist slant (that my Marxist father pointed out to me) in the silent interchange between the feudal old Calcutta honcho (Chhabi Biswas) as he looks down on the little Nepali urchin savouring a whole Cadbury's chocolate—which angers the older man, proud of his affluence and his power.

From *Apur Sansar*, all I carried away was a giant crush on Soumitra Chatterjee, who a malicious friend pointed out with glee, had recently married his lady love. Many years later, I met him many times and built up a sort of warm acquaintanceship. And learnt a lot about the director who discovered him: Satyajit Ray.

From this point on, I began to realise a hunger within me to meet this tall man in person and comment on this film. I went hunting for his postal address and today, I have no memory of how I finally managed to get it. But before that, *Mahanagar (1963)* had released in Lotus and I wrote down my own critique of the film—a very raw one when I look back—and wanted to send it to Ray himself. The theatre drew a full house, surprising for a Bombay audience.

I hesitantly took out my fountain pen—and penned a letter to him. I analysed *Mahanagar* briefly, focusing on the points that appealed to me. I also asked him why he was not making a film on *Pagla Dashu*, a book for children authored by his late father, Sukumar Roy. Pagla Dashu is the hero of a series of stories revolving round his antics. He is a very funny boy on the surface but the undercurrent shows, he is very diabolic in his mischief and naughtiness. The small stories of his adventures are confined to the school he attends and there are different kinds of digs at the teachers and the education system per se.

He replied, saying that he shared with me our Economics background, though he dropped out of Presidency College mid-way. 'I think a man's true education begins after he steps out of his institution. I read much more than I read when I was a student,' he wrote. 'I have met your parents already. Why have I not met you yet? Perhaps, we will meet the next time,' he wrote.

He said that he had just finished his work on *Nastaneer* and lamented that the producer had insisted on changing the name of the film to *Charulata*. 'Thankfully, they did not ask to make any changes in the story,' he said, adding that it was not possible to picturise *Pagla Dashu* because the potshots taken at the education system would not go down well with the powers-that-be. He expressed his plan to make a documentary on the danseuse Bala Saraswati. 'I had gone to watch her recital in Calcutta recently and was stunned with the excellence in performing. I went to the dressing room to meet her after the performance to tell her that I wanted to make a documentary on her. She said, "I am so ugly, why do you want to make a film on me?"'

A few weeks later, he sent two-page reply in an envelope with my name and address written in his unique handwriting. Ma and I were pleasantly surprised. His son said that he always made it a point to answer every single letter he received and also penned the address on the envelope in his own hand.

I visited the family once at 3, Lake Temple Road and was

welcomed quite warmly. Sandip was about ten years old then. His father showed me his *Kheror Khata* in which he wrote his famous scripts in a notebook bound with a red cloth like the grocer's account books of the time. The ten-year-old Sandip did the same in a smaller version of his father's notebook and the father showed it very proudly to me. Ray also handed me his own notebook, filled with sketches of the characters, the costumes he had planned they would wear and small rectangular frames within each page to illustrate his conception of each scene! I was too raw to understand the technicalities but his close attention to the slightest detail was amazing. I hardly looked at the written script, so mesmerised was I with the sketches, including even the footwear the characters would be wearing.

Many years later, while writing my book on Aparna Sen's films, she had given me all her original scripts to study. Except for the sketches, I could clearly see reflected in her films the deep influence of Ray on her directorial work.

Over the years, though we had gone our own ways, I had begun to write generally on cinema and specifically on films I felt might go down in the history of Indian cinema. The influence of Ray on me as a lover of cinema, however, did not spoil me for mainstream films, in general and Hindi cinema, in particular. After all, I was a strange blend of Bombaiya tastes and Bengali culture in food and language. I loved Hindi cinema as much as I adored my Ray and my Sen and my Ritwik Ghatak and Tapan Sinha. Bimal Roy remains very close to my heart as much as Ray does. Strangely, Bimal Roy followed the same practice though they hardly knew each other and there were years between them. In Bimal Roy's cinema, I could catch a glimpse of his discipline, his focus, his complete honesty of purpose towards his work and his closeness with his family.

There is one anecdote I cannot resist narrating. When I got married in 1965 and shifted to Kolkata, my in-laws would poke me for being a 'film journalist' which, in those years, was looked down upon as very low in the hierarchy of journalism. My brother-in-law, then 19, challenged me to call up Ray in front of him. I did, my heart beating fast in case I failed to get Ray on the phone. He took the call himself and I, all of 21, was thrilled. My brother-in-law was stunned!

Soon after this, I began writing a very long history on Bengali cinema for a competition announced by Calcutta University. I got stuck in my research and called Ray up for help. He said the book *Indian Film* jointly authored by Erik Barnouw and S Krishnaswamy would be a very good frame of reference, adding that it was out of print. 'If you want to borrow my copy, you can pick it up from my house and give it back to me after your work is over.' Off I went to his home then at 1/1A Bishop Lefroy Road, where he lived till he passed away.

He sat me down in the lounge, smiled and brought out the book. I touched it reverently as if it was the Bhagwad Gita and after some small talk, left. The competition remained an unfinished history. I did not feel like giving the book back but had to honour my word. The book details the way he would handle the camera or direct his cinematographers, written very simply. Many years later, I noticed the same book in the library of a journalism school in Mumbai where I taught. I flicked the book and still hold it as one of my precious possessions in my film library.

A very young friend of mine, Arindam Saha Sardar, has created a digital archive of original letters written by great celebrities from different fields in his suburban home. I have gifted Satyajit Ray's letters to this archive and he is taking very good care of them.

Ray and I exchanged four letters in all, making a grand total of eight. I misplaced one of them while shifting house. In the last letter, he informs me that my mother had left behind her spectacle case with some cash inside. He asked me if he could send it by money order and I wrote a short response in the affirmative. The money arrived at my mother's place in due course.

I tried to see him once in his Bishop Lefroy Road residence when he was quite unwell. By then, the Marxist government had constructed an elevator that opened right outside the entrance to his second floor residence. The security guard refused me entry, saying 'Visitors are not allowed.' Looking back, I feel it was good I was turned away because I would not want to remember that 6'4' tall, dark and handsome man with that bass voice now a ghost of his former self, relaxing in his study minus his cigarette or pipe. It is good to fall back on the good memories of a man who lived life and cinema on his own terms, setting out some invisible rules for people like me to follow, or at least try.

THE HUNGER TRILOGY

AFFLUENT CULTURES SHOW food beautified in the form of still life paintings and sculpture. In Indian literature, art, film and drama, the focus on food and hunger differs from that in the Western cultural space. In the last century, the common practice was to blame British colonial rule for the massive scarcity of food. After independence, the onus is on whichever political party is in power—not because food is physically scarce but because there is tremendous inequality in its distribution. This leads to scarcity followed by steep rise in prices, resulting in starvation and death. Even today, 80 million Indians live below the poverty line.

Hunger finds a prominent place in three films by Satyajit Ray in different forms and with completely different backdrops. That explains why Ray chose Bibhuti Bhushan Bandopadhyay's works for four films, including his trilogy. Unlike in the West, hunger forms a significant sub-plot in these cinematic narratives, each one, a 'period' piece in a manner of speaking. One is *Pather Panchali*, the second is *Goopy Gayen Bagha Bayen* and the third is *Ashani Sanket*.

PATHER PANCHALI AN EMPTY VESSEL

Hunger is the predominant theme in *Pather Panchali.* A dented brass vessel that the doddering old aunt Indir Thakrun carries with her symbolises the abject despair of the old woman's impoverished, unwanted life. Indir is introduced with a close-up of a brass bowl filled with mish-mash to track back and show the bent old toothless lady eating from the bowl. The vessel she uses for drinking water later symbolises her tragic death as it tumbles down the stones noisily, suggesting that she is no more.

While she is alive, her nephew's wife Sarbajaya and the two kids–Apu and Durga–love her 'not so much because she is their aunt, as because she represents a mysterious force of life and death that fascinates them through her stories of the witch and other fairy tales. It is only when her own children's survival is at stake that Sarbajaya turns her face against the old woman, and she dies like an animal.'[1]

Interestingly, Ray does not focus on this brass vessel much as the story unfolds, so we do not pay attention to it either. It is only when she dies and it tumbles down the rough slope with the unwitting touch of Durga that the camera closes in and follows its movement till it splashes into the water, and we see that it is badly dented, much like the life of its owner. It drowns when its owner dies, as unceremoniously as Indir Thakrun does. In one scene, Sarbajaya sees her sneak into the kitchen. When she comes out, Sarbajaya asks her what she is doing. Indir shows her two green chillies. Durga, who is fond of the old woman, offers her a brinjal.

In another scene, Indir Thakrun returns to Harihar's home from a relative's house. She asks for water when Sarbajaya is having lunch. The younger woman asks her to get it herself as she has the brass vessel with her. Indir fills water, waits for a few minutes watching Sarbajaya eating, flashes a toothless smile in the faint hope that the younger woman might give her something. But when this does not happen, her smile disappears. She moves away, pours the water into the ground, emptying it. Asking for water was just an excuse to get some food. This time, the dented vessel becomes an 'agency' for her to express the pain of rejection, loneliness, alienation.

On two occasions, Sarbajaya throws her out of the house. Each time, she packs her belongings—a tattered straw mat she lies on and a small, dirty wretched bundle that spells out its own story. When she comes back the second time, we see her walking with a stick for support and wearing a weather-beaten shawl. Sarbajaya rebukes her for having 'begged' for the shawl but does not take it away from her. Within Harihar's poverty-stricken family, Indir Thakrun's position is the worst because no one quite wants her around except Durga. Apu is too little to understand what relationships are all about.

Pather Panchali is scattered with items of food. Little Durga hides a guava she has stolen from the Mukherjees' garden inside an earthen pot under a bunch of bananas. When Apu attends the village school in the grocer's shop, we find him drinking milk from a big bowl; as he finishes it, some milk trails down the corners of his mouth. We never see Durga drinking milk. In the shop laden with different items of raw and ready-to-eat food, a little girl arrives to ask for a paisa worth of puffed rice. A visitor arrives at the shop and after some small talk, manages to inveigle a small bottle of cooking oil from the grocer for free. Just before the famous train sequence, we find Durga chewing on a stick of sugarcane. She hands a piece to Apu later on as they walk through the kash fields towards the sound of the approaching train.

Durga is another character fond of snatching whatever item she can, especially food. She listens neither to the warnings of the Mukherjees nor to her mother's threats and keeps stealing guavas and raw mangoes from their garden. She makes a pickle-like mix and shares it with Apu on the sly, warning him not to tell their mother. With her friends, she organises a festive 'picnic' near their house during which the children cook real khichuri[2] over a wooden fire, after a spat over who was to bring the salt and the cooking oil. Food, its material and allegorical qualities, its physical and time-bound consumption and appropriation play a critically significant role in poor and lower middle-class rural Indian families even today.

In one scene, Sarbajaya asks Durga to fetch molasses for two paisa because she wants to make payesh[3] for Apu. Durga knows it is only for her brother but the preference given to her little brother is normalised by her. She loves him very much. The famous scene where she eggs Apu on to follow the sweet vendor with his treasure trove right to the home of her affluent friend is another example of her craving for food. The children are enjoying the fragrance of the sweets and following him in the hope that wherever he goes, they might get to sample some. The stray dog follows them and we see their shadows in the pond running beside the muddy road. Does this mean that Durga is a glutton? No, it is clear that she craves food all the time because she is deprived of basic food. Sneaking into the neighbour's garden fills her hunger and simultaneously brings some adventure into her bleak life.

The references to all kinds of food—not the modern, manufactured, packaged, sophisticated brand but organic food

(cereal, vegetables, fruit, milk, molasses, rice, puffed rice, spinach) in *Pather Panchali* does not have a decorative value but subtly highlights the underlining theme of poverty in Harihar's family accompanied by decay and hunger in its varied manifestations. The film is black-and-white so the food remains stripped of the glamour of colour. One does not find Apu stealing fruits, only Durga does it. Only once in the entire film do we hear of the fish Harihar has bought home from the market. The allegories bring out poverty, making us wonder whether the lives of Sarbajaya, Harihar and Apu will ever be free of it.

The 'objects' in the film too symbolise hunger and poverty leading to degraded human lives: from the tattered shawl of Indir Thakrun with a huge hole in the middle, through the chain of beads Durga stole from her friend, the tattered sari Sarbajaya wears when there is no news from Harihar for five long months and nothing in the house to eat.

In *Pather Panchali*, food is so visibly and verbally significant that it throws in relief the lack of other concrete objects of use or nostalgia that are subtly present. One example is the hand-fan Sarbajaya uses to fan the burning embers of her earthen oven, or to shoo away disturbing elements, to fan her husband Harihar when he sits down for lunch, and only once, to fan herself as she rests on the earthen floor of the small compound.

For Sarbajaya's family, their lives revolve around the uncertainty of food in everyday lives. When no food is left, we find Sarbajaya digging out some brass plates and a bowl at the break of dawn to pawn off secretly so that she can buy food for the children. This is captured through a collage of shots without dialogue but with natural sounds of the vessels being taken out, the door being shut and Sarbajaya walking out and coming back.

This hunger expressed through food is gender-specific. Apu plays with the stray dog; he is fed fondly by his mother and shows little interest in eating because it is 'only rice.' He shapes a paper crown adorned with silver paper he stole from Durga's toy box and runs around playing king. The makeshift moustache comes off but the crown remains. He is imitating the persona of the king in the jatra performance he watched the previous night.

Sarbajaya is left to deal single-handedly with poverty in its scariest extreme. The one time we see Harihar eating, his plate is filled with a small 'hillock' of rice while his wife fans him with a hand-held fan. Yet, the camera rarely closes in on items of food or dwells on them only in passing. For example, in the picnic scene, we see that something is being cooked, which is later eaten but we never get to see visuals of the actual dish.

The one scene that shows Sarbajaya having lunch, the camera keeps away from the act of eating and keeps it in suggestion focusing on Indir Thakrun's face. There are constant hints, if one can catch them, about the consumption of food or rather, the lack of proper and adequate food shown only through Durga's childish pranks of stealing fruit or following the sweet vendor on his journey. During Durga Pooja, there is a shot where children crowd around when prasad is being handed out from a big basket, as was normal in Bengal villages at the time.

When Indir Thakrun dies, little Apu follows the hearse to

the burning ghat while the soundtrack plays a song the deceased sang when she was alive. This song was rendered by the old actress Chunibala herself that went: *Haridin to gelo, sandhya holo, paar koro amaare* (The day has passed and evening has set in, help me to get across.) What a song, what a rendering and what a moving performance!

ASHANI SANKET A CELLULOID CRITIQUE ON MANUFACTURED HUNGER

Most film critics, cinema scholars and historians tried to establish that Satyajit Ray did not make political films or did not even subtly suggest his political leanings. He himself never stated that his films were political. However, looking at his body of work, much of it inspired, adapted and rooted in literary origins, spells out a different reading decades after his films first hit the screen.

Ray decided to make *Ashani Sanket* (Distant Thunder, 1973) in colour, his first after *Kanchenjunga*. The original story, written by Bibhutibhushan Bandopadhyay is more a prognosis of the 1943 famine than a depiction of the famine itself. The film focuses on the impact of the famine on people of rural Bengal where food is unavailable not because there has been a scarcity in farm produce but because the British rulers are stocking up foodgrain for soldiers after war broke out; the blue sky filled with beautiful clouds is soon filled with fighter planes, spreading panic. But the poor masses do not understand the ramifications of the war on their lives.

The illiterate and semi-literate villagers do not really understand why this is happening, much less the logic of a man-made famine. Their entire focus is on dealing with hunger and the situation becomes tragic when cholera breaks out in the village and people begin to die, either of starvation or of cholera.

Amartya Sen received his Nobel Prize mainly on the strength of his work on famines and the book *Poverty and Famines*, which had a chapter on the 'Great Bengal Famine'. It began with the following premise:

> Starvation is the characteristic of some people not having enough food to eat. It is not the characteristic of there being not enough food to eat. While the latter can be a cause of the former, it is but one of many possible causes. Whether and how starvation relates to food supply is a matter for factual investigation.[4]

Sen argued in his other works that food availability in 1943 was 'at least 11 per cent higher than in 1941 when there was nothing remotely like a famine'.[5]

The film is set in a village in Bengal during World War II. The story is narrated from the life and struggles of Gangacharan (Soumitra Chatterjee) and examines the effect of the the great famine on the village of Bengal. Gangacharan settles in the remote village of Natungaon as its only Brahmin, becoming its

self-styled doctor, so-called ceremonial priest and elementary school head, with his sensitive wife, Ananga (Babita) by his side. He dispenses 'medical' advice though he hardly has much knowledge of it. He and Ananga are content in their small pocket of happiness. Ananga does not quite like the way he fools people and asks them for a 'price' in kind but he gloats over it so she keeps quiet.

Ray remained faithful to the spirit of the story though he does take creative liberty. Gangacharan, the lone Brahmin in a remote village, lives off the gullibility of the ignorant and illiterate villagers who are either peasants or labourers in awe of him and he boasts about it to his pretty wife. He is 'paid' in kind by the villagers who respect him and have faith in him, which enables the couple to enjoy material comforts.

The shock comes suddenly when the villagers hear that rice has become scarce, not really aware that this is a man-made scarcity and not a natural one. The camera swiftly moves to massive bags of grains being secretly hoarded by the only wholesaler of rice in the village to be later sold in the black market. The villagers are forced to beg and borrow without much succour. They loot the wholesaler's shop and godown and he is forced to stock his rice in his home where he lives with his young widowed daughter. On one occasion, the looters beat him up, nearly taking his life. This violence unleashed by goons who loot the rice, looked at holistically, is much less than the violence inflicted on the villagers by the British rulers who force the people they are supposed to take care of starve to death.

Even Ananga, now pregnant, goes with Chhutki (Sandhya Roy), a neighbour who is very fond of her, to dig arum roots from the watery bushes and overgrown weeds to boil for food. The pregnant Ananga is attacked by a man while collecting the roots but the very bold and angry Chhutki attacks the molester with the instrument she was digging the arum roots with. Ray never allows the camera to show the face of the molester even when he dies because of the terrible attack on him by Chhukti.

Gangacharan goes to the wholesale grain merchant to ask for some rice. The merchant refuses but says that as Gangacharan is a Brahmin, he is invited to have lunch in his home and then leave. He has to cook it himself because he is Brahmin and no one can cook for him. But he does not have the faintest clue about cooking. The wholesaler's young widowed daughter stands beside him and instructs him. When the food is ready, looking at the 'tempting' spread, Gangacharan remembers his pregnant wife Ananga at home and gets up without eating. The young widow helps him exit through a back door, hands him some rice and other food items and implores him to approach her if he needs more. A small touch of humanity in an ambience filled with hunger and starvation is beautiful without being melodramatic.

Through the minor characters in the village juxtaposed against the sole Brahmin, Ray subtly and repeatedly underscores the heavy weight with which casteism bears down on people even in a situation where starvation prevails. Though his Brahmin identity was a boon for him, now, in the changed scenario, Gangacharan's world collapses around him. Ray shows the human scale of a man-made disaster that killed more than five million people. The film unfolds at a leisurely pace that reflects the rhythms of village life, but gathers speed as the traditional village norms undergo an unimaginable catharsis under the pressure of starvation and death.

Ashani Sanket depicts the disastrous impact of World War II on the rural life of Bengal. Juxtaposing the plight of Bengal's villagers against the backdrop of war and famine, the novel and the film both unfold, slowly and surely, the suffering of helpless villagers in the absence of any kind of historical agency or participation in the actual process. The theme of famine has been explored with more power and sharpness by Mrinal Sen in *Matira Manasha* (Two Brothers, 1966). This same issue has been subject of a number of plays by the Indian People's Theatre Association. The most prominent example is *Nabanna* (New Crop) by Bijan Bhattacharya. Director Khwaja Ahmad Abbas's famous Hindi film *Dharti ke Lal* (Children of the Earth, 1946) too is set against the backdrop of the famine.

This writer had the opportunity of watching the IPTA production of *Nabanna* at a theatre conference in Bombay as a little girl. Both Ritwik Ghatak and Bijon Bhattacharya acted in the play but I did not understand much of what was going on except that everyone was very poor, wearing old and torn clothes and dying of hunger. Understandably, I did not like the performance at all, unaware of what I had missed, not unnatural for a girl of eight. This play shows the miserable condition the uprooted people from Bengal villages were undergoing in the urban milieu.

Nimai Ghosh's *Chhinnamul* (The Uprooted, 1950) was about the partition of Bengal, about the harrowing lives of the people who, in its aftermath, acquired the label of 'refugee.' Its unique element was its heavy accent on realism. It was unique in its narrative force, fluid camera movements, deft handling of actors sans make-up, effective use of dialects of East and West Bengal and extensive location shooting. Ghosh ushered neo-realism in Indian cinema before Ray rediscovered it in *Pather Panchali* (1955) and Bimal Roy reinvented it in *Do Bigha Zamin* (1953.)

Most memorable in *Chhinnamul* was the gruesome scene at Sealdah railway station showing refugees from East Bengal swarming Calcutta (now Kolkata) in great numbers. As they lay huddled on railway platforms, they were plagued with poverty, squalor and epidemics. There were rotting corpses too. Ghosh visited the spot with his crew to film the scene. His actors, slovenly dressed to match the refugees, shuffled through the crowd. By concealing the camera in a van stationed nearby, Ghosh shot them in that difficult location. A young man approached him requesting to be given a role in the film and was given him the role of a refugee. The man who made his debut in this manner later focused his films on the uprooting of East Bengalis and the social, emotional and financial trauma they had to undergo as a consequence. His name was Ritwik Ghatak.

Ashani Sanket was perhaps Ray's first venture into a very historically significant film with a political statement that emphasises how scarcity of food that leads on one hand, to the black-marketing of grains in the home market, and on the other, creates hunger, starvation, divisionism and violence among those who cannot afford to buy it. The then British rulers were not bothered at all and Ray sometimes subtly and sometimes powerfully suggests how this impacted the traditional values the villagers had grown up with.

Chhutki is a healthy-looking young woman who declares, 'I am always hungry.' Among the ways and means to fulfill her hunger is trading sex for food. Her hunger gets the better of her when she decides to run away with the scar-faced brick kiln worker who has been inducing her to go to the city with him. Nothing is said out loud but everything is achieved through suggestion. Chhutki, once a bubbly, proud, fiery village belle, is reduced to a ghost of herself. When Ananga gets angry with her, she retorts, 'Hunger, my dear sister, hunger. I will get food in the city.' Whether she really staved off hunger in the city or not, one thing is sure—she will never come back.

Moti's situation is different. When everyone in the village is either dying of starvation or running away, she lies dying for days at a stretch. Yet, before she talks about food, she warns Ananga not to touch her as 'You will have to take a bath, then,' because she is untouchable, a Dalit. Caste barriers overshadow her terrifying hunger. In her dying moments, she craves 'hot rice, fish curry and a vegetable mishmash.' When Ananga brings some arum root folded with a banana leaf, she is too weak to even touch it. A little girl standing behind a slender bush waits for the woman to die so that she can dart out and pick up the banana leaf bundle. The camera wanders across two butterflies and a grasshopper, features of Nature oblivious to the tragedy within the human world. As soon as Moti dies, the little girl runs out to pick up the banana leaf which Moti did not even touch.

If Moti dies due to scarcity of food, Chhutki turns her body into an 'object' for consumption by others in the city hungering to satisfy their basic instincts. These two disparate repercussions of the man-made famine on two different women reveal the underbelly of hunger among the starving masses. Moti's death also reflects the cruel reality of the caste system where no one in the village will touch her dead body to consign it to flames. Gangacharan breaks tradition by handling her body for burial which, being a devout Brahmin, he is not supposed to do. 'More than five million people died of starvation and epidemics in Bengal in what came to be known as the man-made famine in 1943' is the message on the screen as the film ends.

Ray was roundly criticised for making the film in glamorous colour and for showing on wispy clouds floating against an azure blue sky, showing the lovely village landscape as famine stalks the land. The answer to this is that Ray may have used colour to sharply underline the contrast between the beautiful colours of Nature and the browns and ambers and ochres and starkness of the lives of hungry human beings. 'There is nothing wrong in the climate, the seasons, the flora and the fauna' the film seems to say. 'But still, there is no colour left in the lives of the villagers. What they face are death and destruction over which they have no control.'

The other critique is about the peaches-and-cream skin of Ananga who also sports plucked eyebrows throughout the film. The slow and steady descent into poverty and lack of food in their life does not seem to have much bearing on her beauty. However, there are dark circles around her eyes and her expression is filled with sadness.

The film comes to a dramatic end when a poor Brahmin who would often join Gagancharan for a sumptuous lunch followed by an afternoon siesta visits with his family from a neighbouring village. Shot against the sinking sun and captured in silhouette, the crowd walking with him grows till one sees hundreds of starving villagers from neighbouring places arriving in search of food.

Can anyone say *Ashani Sanket* is not a political film? It is a brilliant adaptation of a classic piece of Bengali literature, true. But it is also a very important political film that stands the test of time and transcends its literary moorings.

GOOPY GAYEN BAGHA BAYEN
DANCE OF GHOSTS, HUNGER AND MAGIC

Those who have loved *Goopy Gayen Bagha Bayen* will be surprised to learn that the film almost never got made because Satyajit Ray found it difficult to get a producer. When the Duttas got roped in, they kept the budget low at Rs 6 lakh, so the film could not be made in colour, which would have perhaps added a new dimension to the fantasy fairytale. The casting posed another problem because the actors Ray originally wanted were not affordable.

The film was based on an illustrated four-page story created by Ray's paternal grandfather, Upendrakishore Roy Choudhury, an internationally known printer who had innovated several printing techniques unknown at the time and also wrote beautiful stories for children. The story was first published in his children's magazine *Sandesh* in 1915. Ray made a few changes in the original script to suit his conception. *Goopy Gayen Bagha Bayen* turned out to be the greatest commercial hit among Ray's entire oeuvre, having a run of fifty-one straight weeks in West Bengal theatres.

Goopy Gayen Bagha Bayen revolves around two simple souls. Goopy lives in a village called Amloki and Bagha is an orphan from Hortuki village. Both names are drawn from a sour fruit which also has medicinal uses. Goopy dreams of becoming a great singer but he cannot really sing. Bagha loves to play the dhol but he too, like Goopy is no musical genius. Heeding the advice of village elders, Goopy wakes up early in the morning to sing a morning raga in front of the king's palace. The king angrily breaks his tanpura and orders their expulsion from the village riding a donkey. Goopy's poor father wipes a tear but can do nothing to save his son from this humiliation.

These two lost souls find themselves on the edge of a forest where, frightened by a tiger, Goopy begins to sing out of tune to shoo the tiger away. The tiger disappears but the forest suddenly becomes very dark and both Goopy and Bagha see dark, shadowy, small figures in silhouette. They are ghosts. Suddenly, the darkness of the night is broken with the appearance of a five-point star with twinkling lights and the ghost king makes his appearance. He takes kindly to the two simpletons and tells them he can give them three boons. A startled Goopy and Bagha ask that they should get food and clothes of their choice, that they travel as and when and where they desire; the third wish is that they should be able to mesmerise their listeners with the magic of their music.

Ray uses magical effects in sound, music and visuals to

bring to life the ghost king who talks in a mechanical voice. Ray lends his own voice to the king, using a tape recorder to make it sound as if it emerges from a machine. The king talks in a sing-song tone and has a smiling mask on his face which disarms Goopy and Bagha. To make their first wish come true, they must give each other a 'high five' with one palm. For the second wish, the King magically produces a pair of beautifully crafted slippers which both must share to be able to travel anywhere and everywhere. For the third wish, well, they test themselves and miraculously, Goopy finds that he can sing with excellent command over raga and tala and Bagha can play the drum very well too.

Most memorable is a seven-minute dance of ghosts performed to several kinds of percussion instruments drawn from the South. This is a technical innovation and socio-political comment at the same time. There are four different kinds of ghosts. The first group appears in a line, shadowy, willowy silhouettes dressed in white that look like badly made paper cut-outs dancing to Kathakali poses. The second row in black silhouette comprises of figures representing a collage of soldiers, peasants, and so on. The third row is filled with mask-wearing British rulers of different designations indicated by the hats they wear; all of them wear masks, walk stiffly with arched backs, some have walking sticks too. The men in the fourth row have huge stomachs and form a microcosm of the capitalist exploiters in society—the Brahmin priest, the Christian priest, the fat-bellied businessman, the moneylender, and so on. These rows are symbiotic in the beginning but as they reappear in two more frames, they begin to fight among themselves. You observe a fat-bellied man wearing a striped kurta handing over some money to the Brahmin priest who pockets it at once. The Christian clergyman thrusts the Bible at the others, forcing them to read. This may appear very entertaining and funny, especially for children, but if one probes deeper, one can read Ray's socio-political comment on the caste-class schism in society.

Ray, who himself designed the costumes for the entire film, paid special attention to the costumes, headgear and hairstyle of the ghosts, though they were shadowy figures in the first row and become sharper as the hierarchy rises. The masks close to the camera have bulging eyes, especially one among the British ghosts. Ray maintained an entire sketchbook of costumes of the ghosts. One cannot stop wondering whether the shadowy ghosts were real dancers or man-made puppets because the dance itself is beautifully choreographed and performed. We have never seen anything like this before or after.

Hunger is a parallel story that runs alongside the tale of two innocent villagers blessed by three wonderful boons. Their first boon is granted in the form of two huge, decorated circular silver plates surrounded by beautifully curved silver bowls that suddenly appear before them. One by one, items of food fill up the two plates and the two begin to dig into the food at once. This is one side of the story. The food in fact, is so much and so varied that the two forever hungry souls soon leave their silver plates while Goopy throws some leftovers at a waiting hungry dog. This perhaps suggests that even the desperately hungry can throw food away and give it literally to the dogs.

Once Goopy and Bagha use their magic to mesmerise their audience, they begin on their adventurous journey first to Halla and then to Shundi, ruled by kings who are identical twins. The king of Halla is constantly drugged by his evil prime minister with the help of the court magician Borfi—a brilliant cameo by the late Harindranath Chattopadhyay. The drugs push the king into fits of violence and childish behaviour. We see him doing some origami with paper in one scene while in another, he jumps out of his throne to fight an invisible enemy when the prime minister cries '*Juddho!*' (War!). In other words, the king is effectively suppressed by the prime minister but does not know it. The prime minister keeps the subjects, soldiers, court employees and prison guards starving; even the camels reserved for war are kept hungry.

Shundi presents a different story altogether. The subjects mingle in the marketplace happily, their religion identifiable by the caps they wear or don't wear. They are all mute due to a plague that attacked the entire population; the king was away with his family so he is not mute. But he refuses to talk because his subjects cannot. He does not believe in any line of defence so Shundi has no army, no weaponry, no defence minister and no war strategy. This makes it very simple for the evil prime minister of Halla to wage war against Shundi so that he can rule over both Halla and Shundi. The king of Shundi who appointed Goopy and Bagha as court musicians after they won the music contest appeals to them to go to Halla, rescue his brother and stop the war.

Ray stresses on the hungry faces sharply and repeatedly

to show the tremendous suffering among everyone in the kingdom of Halla, including the soldiers. In one scene, the king's cruel, cold-blooded minister bites a chicken leg as a prison guard stares hungrily at him; the minister asks, 'Why are you so greedy, man?' The appearance of the guard—skinny, skeletal with hollowed out cheeks, his expression and his bent body—spell out that he has probably not eaten for days. in another scene, the messenger, portrayed by Chinmoy Roy, says with a toothless smile, 'I have not eaten for days, Sir.'

When war is declared between Halla and Shundi, Ray needed an 'army' of junior artistes to create the scene. How would he manage such a huge crowd of skeletal people with deeply burrowed eyes and hollow cheeks? Ray decided to take his team to Rajasthan to shoot the war sequences. The spot chosen was a desert without a single plant or tree in sight. The only people wandering across the desert were camel riders of a nomadic community. These gypsies had no water to drink and the only food they had access to were roundels of dry bread and a chunk of jaggery.

It was an extremely hungry community starved of food. So, when they were asked to appear in the film as soldiers of Halla's army, they agreed at once when they were told that there would be lots of very good food.[6] When the shots of pots of sweets falling from the skies were taken, they pounced on the food and the shots had almost the effect of a documentary film though the audience remained unaware of this. This was a strange and tragic intersection between the reel and the real. The war scenes in this sense, define a situation where two different kinds of history have merged—the history of real hunger with the history of a film that carried a strong undercurrent of hunger. But does this not mean the filmmaker exploited a large group of very hungry people to make his war scenes realistic? What happened to those hungry gypsies after the shoot was over? No one knows.

Through a beautifully edited sequence, we see the child-like king of Halla grabbing an earthen pot filled with *rosogullas* given to him by Goopy and Bagha after the war. They want to take him to his brother in Shundi. He keeps gobbling up one large-sized *rosogulla* after another in a very un-kingly manner. This is perhaps an indicator that he too, was deprived of good food. Goopy and Bagha pick him up and the scene immediately shifts to the three of them landing in Shundi's court while the king of Halla unaware of his surroundings, devours his *rosogullas* with great joy.

Stopping the war even before it has begun is a cakewalk for Goopy and Bagha, who begin to sing; their music has a hypnotic effect on the soldier, the prime minister and the king. They then wish for sweets like *rosogullas*, *chamcham*, *sandesh* and so on and extra-large sweets begin dropping from the skies above. The hungry soldiers pounce on these earthen pots and the war comes to an end before it can begin. The king sprints down the steps of the place shouting '*Chhutti chhutti chhutti*' like a little child freed from captivity after a long time. Goopy and Bagha hold him between them while he is the earthen pot of *rosogullas*. The king is not even aware that he is already in Shundi because he is busy eating. The Shundi King keeps his promise of offering his daughter's hand to Goopy. When Bagha is sad because Shundi's daughter is too tall for him, the Halla king offers his daughter who is the right size. The screen turns to colour when the two silent, veiled beauties appear on the scene with Goopy and Bagha in princely attire.

Ray not only took technical innovations in cinema to a new dimension with *Goopy Gayen Bagha Bayen* but also with the lyrics of the songs, which were written and composed by Ray himself. For example, in the ghost song which Goopy sings and Bagha plays the drums, they describe the kind of ghosts they have come to know of such as—thin, fat, narrow, chubby, straight, crooked, lame and blind—as a thanksgiving song after getting the boons. The one they sing in the Shundi court goes: *Maharaja tomaake shelam, mora Bangladesher thekey elaam* (King, we bow to you, from the land of Bangladesh which we come from). This shakes the king out of the deep slumber the other classical singers had pushed him into and he begins to sway to the beat. The anti-war song is *O rey Halla rajar shena, tora juddho korey korbi kee ta bol* (O my dear soldiers of Halla king, tell us what will you gain through war?) Each song has a special place in the film also in terms of its picturisation and choreography so you cannot remember the film without its songs.

Ray had originally thought of Kishore Kumar to lend his voice to the songs of Goopy but he had date problems so Ray chose Anup Ghoshal, an outstanding classical singer. The biting satire contained in the lyrics, music and delivery of the song targeting the prime minister has been conceived with some original beats: *Oh Montri moshai shodojontri mosha, tobe thaak* (Oh minister, the diabolic one, let it be). This is the song they sing to escape from prison.

As for members of the cast, they deserve special mention. Tapen Chatterjee made his debut as Goopy and as he had no star image, he simply melted into the character. Robi Ghosh was already an established character actor and he had no problems essaying Bagha with the comments he makes when Goopy sings and his fetish of washing his hands before every meal even when very hungry. Forgotten comedians of Bengali cinema such as Jahar Roy as the prime minister, Haridhan Mukherjee as a village elder and Nripati Chatterjee as the skeletal prison guard, among others, give masterly performances. Santosh Dutta as the twin kings of Halla and Shundi performs extremely well. The performances are so organic that they seem to flow naturally.

Though it is now common knowledge that Ray made *Goopy Gayen Bagha Bayen* for children because of his son's wish, today it comes across as much a film for adults. It offers everything equated with entertainment in cinema and at the same time, throws up a political essay on hunger and its ramifications in the modern world where in India, leaders like to sustain poverty because it forces the poor to vote and keeps the size of the electorate rising. The poor always expect that whoever comes to power will take care of their hunger—basic, physical hunger sometimes bordering on starvation.

At the other end of the spectrum, the film shows how hunger can be used to stop a war even before it begins. When *rosogullas* rain from the heavens above, the war goes to the dogs and all the starving soldiers rush to collect the earthen pots and begin to gobble up as much as they can, including the king of Shundi. Another angle is that every state needs to maintain a minimum line of defence so that it can defend itself and its people from war-mongering neighbours. Peace does not mean the total absence of self-defence for without preparation, the state will lose the war much before it has begun.

As urban elites enjoy their plush limousines and air-conditioners, indulge in a more diversified diet and reduce the resulting adipose tissue in slimming clinics, little do they concern themselves about how the neo-liberal policies that have benefited them have, at the same time, enmeshed millions of their country-men and women in deep debt and land loss, reducing their lives to a struggle to survive as humans. A former government's insistence on hunger and starvation being a 'voluntary choice' reminds one of one Marie Antoinette who, before the French Revolution, had advised her starving subjects to have cake if there was no bread.

This critic's only grouse about this film is the total marginalisation of the two princesses—the daughters of Shundi and Halla—who are reduced to dumb, doll-like appearances and are not permitted to say a word for or against the choice of illiterate, poor and plain-looking villagers as their husbands. Shundi's king remains mute because his subjects cannot speak. But he refuses to grant his daughter a voice of her own.

Endnotes

1. *The Cinema of Satyajit Ray,* Chidananda Dasgupta, Vikas Publishing House, Delhi, 1980, p.22.
2. *Khichuri* is a single dish meal among many Indians, not just Bengalis, a mish-mash of rice, pulses, vegetables, spices and oil.
3. *Payesh* is a Bengali dessert, a kind of rice pudding cooked with molasses and thick milk.
4. *Poverty and Famines: An Essay on Entitlement and Deprivation,* Amartya Sen, OUP, 1983.
5. *Past Continuous: The Deep Impact of the Bengal Famine on the Indian Psyche,* Nilanjan Mukhopadhyay, The Wire, 17 April 2018.
6. *Panchali Thekey Oscar, Part II,* Aniruddha Dhar & Ujjal Chakraborty & Atanu Chakraborty, Pratibhas, Kolkata, 2011, pp. 223-25. Translated from the original by Shoma A Chatterji.

MASCULINITY IN RAY'S FILMS

INDIAN CINEMA IN general reveals a wide variety of masculinity in the male protagonist, from God figures drawn from Hindu mythology to saints derived from the stories of saint poets; from swashbuckling, sword-swinging heroes whose aim is to rescue damsels in distress to the generous, kind-hearted, affectionate and self-sacrificing hero who gives up his love for a greater cause. With rare exceptions, representations of masculinity of the male protagonist in mainstream Hindi cinema has been largely hegemonic because the films and the sources they are traced back to—literature, real life, newspaper clippings, religious icons and historical leaders—have imbibed their values directly from patriarchy, the dominating ideology of the country barring a few matrilineal ethnic groups that began to fade with urbanisation and industrialisation. But these images do not coincide with the masculinities one encounters in Bengali cinema, barring a few exceptions. The male heroes and character artistes in Satyajit Ray's films have constantly stood their ground by refusing to place themselves within any cliched definition of the 'masculine'.

Robert Connell, a pioneer in the study of masculinities[1] put forth for the first time that there are different kinds of masculinities and that one of these is dominant. This came like a beacon in theoretical studies about what made men 'men'. The 'dominant' form of masculinity was defined by Connell as hegemonic masculinity. Other kinds of masculinity were either subsumed or marginalised and hegemonic masculinity was the frame of reference to live up to. The relationship between these different ways to be a man are characterised by conflict faced by most men, often in relation to women.

Since these early theories on masculinity are two decades old, there is hardly any study that explores masculinities in the heroes in Bengali cinema such as Pramathesh Chandra Barua in the 1940s to Uttam Kumar and Soumitra Chatterjee till 1980 and Prosenjit since the 1990s to the present day. Barua created a distinct screen icon of 'masculinity' elaborated on his own terms. Uttam Kumar redefined the concept of masculinity that, placed in perspective, merges into the Bengali *bhadralok* identity that found favour with his audience—male, and female, with equal appeal. Soumitra Chatterjee entered the cinema scenario to tinge the history of Bengali cinema with his evolving a unique brand of masculinity distanced from his predecessor and rival Uttam Kumar's. His screen masculinity is more appropriately placed within post-colonial, independent India though it was 'born' in Satyajit Ray's *Apur Sansar* related to an earlier time in Bengal's history. He still represented the *bhadralok* but in a more refined, subtle, understated and sophisticated form. The screen *bhadralok* in fact, had metamorphosed from Barua's *Devdas* to Uttam Kumar's *Harano Sur* to Soumitra Chatterjee's *Saat Pake Bandha*. None of these heroes bared their bodies to show off their six abs, did not perform action scenes, fight much, use swear words or abusive language, or indulge in aggressive sport activities. They spouted poetry and sang songs. They therefore, neatly fit into the conventional Bengali *bhadralok* persona that led to their massive popularity among and identification with the Bengali audience. These heroes corresponded to the concept of hegemonic masculinity because they turned into live icons to imitate, be fascinated by and to worship.

Is masculinity born, does it evolve over time or is it thrust on the man? Masculinity is not a monolith. It is not a homogenous term that can define all men of all ages across geography, culture, language class and time. It is an abstract, fluid and differential value that attaches itself to men subject to the time they function and live in, the class they belong to, the language they speak and the social ambience they move within, which, interestingly, are also not fixed in time and space. In his paper, *Bengalis but not Men? Bhadralok Masculinities in Adda,*[2] Romit Chowdhury lays bare how masculinities, 'far from being natural, are made in particular socio-cultural contexts.' His paper has 'drawn on literature in the field of masculinity studies to highlight the interactional dynamics through which ideas of *bhadralok* masculinity are produced in a particular form of sociality in contemporary Kolkata.'

Chowdhury insists:

> The colonial discourse in Bengal imposed stereotypes of the 'manly Englishman' and the 'effeminate Bengali as a justification of colonial rule in the region. The colonial construct was that the Bengali *Babu* was sharp of intellect but frail of limbs, a configuration that was internalised by the *bhadralok* himself. Both Barua and Uttam Kumar in their screen personas define an interesting amalgam of the 'manly Englishman' and the 'effeminate Bengali' albeit, in totally different ways.

This brings us to the masculinities seen in the screen personas of firstly, the actors who performed in Ray's films and secondly, the characters they performed on screen. Uttam Kumar, Pahari Sanyal, Soumitra Chatterjee, Victor Banerjee, Anil Chatterjee, Chhabi Biswas, Dhritman Chatterjee, Santosh Dutta, Tapen Chatterjee, Robi Ghosh, Subendu Chatterjee, Barun Chanda, Tulsi Chakraborty, Kali Banerjee, Kanu Bandopadhyay and some others are the actors who featured in films directed by Ray often as hero and sometimes, in important character roles such as Sailen Mukherjee, Shyamal Ghosal, Samit Bhanja among many others.

If one takes a deeper look, one can observe that none of Ray's male characters lend themselves to any stereotypical description—academically defined or sociologically explained—to a homogenous, monolithic description of what constitutes 'masculinity', much less to the socially constructed description of 'macho.'

According to this writer's observations over time, the very concepts of 'macho', 'masculinity' et cetera are codified superimpositions from without by a society dominated by patriarchal modes of thinking where the man, never mind if he is fully clothed and looks like a well-bred, suave gentleman, is ideally defined by the social codes that define 'masculinity.' In this sense, 'masculinity' is a fluid concept that changes from time to time, space to space and culture to culture. Extending the same logic to the heroes, character artists and cameos in Ray's flm, there just cannot be any comparison between Soumitra Chatterjee as Apu in *Apur Sansar* and the same actor as the taxi driver in *Abhijaan*. One cannot draw any parallels between Kali Banerjee in *Monihara* and Kali Banerjee in *Parash Pathar*. Or, take Uttam Kumar as Arindam Mukherjee in *Nayak* and Uttam Kumar as Byomkesh Bakshi in *Chiriakhana*. Ray himself did not believe in villains either.

Amitava Nag writes in the book *Satyajit Ray's Heroes & Heroines*: [3]

> In one of his interviews, Ray categorically mentioned that villains, in general, bore him. What he probably meant was the common depiction of an all-evil person in popular culture, including mainstream cinema and the literature, globally. For him, human beings were more ambivalent and less monochromatic.

According to research by Kausttuv Bakshi:[4]

> The representation of the male body has been extensively discussed in film and media studies in the last few decades. Following Mulvey's (1975) work on the

> representation of the female body, attention has more recently turned to the representation of masculinity, paying particular attention to the male body and critical approaches in exploring the various facets through which masculinity is performed and embodied through the cinematic medium.

'Masculinities' are not the same as 'men'. To speak of masculinities is to speak about gender relations. Masculinities concern the position of men in a gender order. They can be defined as the patterns of practice by which people engage that position. Among the signifiers of masculinity in Bengali actors during the 1940s right into the 1970s, the most predominant is the cultural structure of the Bengali *Bhadralok* which, sadly, today is an inherited culture of our past reduced to ruin and decay but conveniently explained away to globalisation and its contents, or discontents. Today, the *bhadra* has either disappeared or faded from contemporary Bengali heroes who have fiercely retained the *lok* of the earlier term *bhadralok* while the prefix Bangali (Bengali) slowly but surely made place for a more cosmopolitan, crude, colourful, loud and brute screen hero with a hybridised masculinity borrowed from Southern and Bollywood cinema imposed on the 'Bengali' cinema of today. Ray's celluloid men, however, stand apart and define their own identity, NOT masculinity or 'macho' characteristic and like it or not, have come to be defined as 'having acted under the directorial baton of Ray.'

PARASH PATHAR PHILOSOPHICAL TONE

Parash Pathar (The Magic Stone, 1958) has two outstanding back stories which should never be forgotten. One, that of the writer on whose story the film is based. Two, the main actor Tulsi Chakraborty, who portrays the historic role of Paresh Dutta, the protagonist. The story was written by Rajshekhar Basu, who became very famous as Parasuram, his pen name. He was one of the most venerated figures of twentieth century Bengal. He is still known as one of the greatest satirists in Bengali during the post-Tagore era. A leading light of Bengali literature, Rajshekhar was a remarkable personality. He was a chemist by profession but his expertise ranged over the fields of mechanical engineering, cottage industries, linguistics, lexicography and the scriptures. Above all, he was a humorist par excellence, and an astonishingly creative writer. However, though he lived a successful life as a noted chemist, his personal life ended tragically because reportedly, he died in penury. He made fun of his poverty too and never permitted this to spill over into his writing. One of his stories involving his literary creation *Birinchibaba* was picked by Ray for another film *Mahapurush*, which featured in his twin films *Kapurush-Mahapurush*. *Birinchibaba* is perhaps the first literary and cinematic representation of fake babas, so common today.[5]

Tulsi Chakraborty, one of the most talented actors in the history of Bengali cinema, was reduced to very minor comic roles and cameos in films for a pittance as low as Rs 15 for a film. So, when Satyajit Ray offered him Rs 100 for his role in *Parash Pathar*, he begged him to pay less because if word got around, he would be kicked out of the industry. He looked up to Ray as "God" and joined his hands in a *namaskar* whenever he passed a theatre where the film was being screened. He was a naturally gifted actor who did a small cameo in *Pather Panchali* too. He did not believe in wearing make-up for his roles. The story goes that he burst into tears when he heard that Ray had picked him to play the main role in his film.

Ray made significant changes to the original story to fit into the socio-political and economic milieu of Calcutta in the late 1950s. Paresh Chandra Dutta, 53, a bank clerk, finds his services abruptly terminated.

In the original story, Paresh Babu is a lawyer. Ray depicted him as a clerk to essay the real backdrop of the escalating conflict between bank workers and their employers for better pay scales. The graphic design of the film, conceived and executed by Ray himself, consists of two diamonds, one white and one black. This throws up the contrast between two

diametrically opposite values—evil and good. Basic ethical and universal values are symbolised by the magic stone in the film.

The script traces Paresh Babu's relationship with this stone that changes the socio-economic map of his life, his network and raises him to a social platform he could never have imagined in normal course. Narrated in the style of a docu-fiction, with a voice-over stepping in to narrate some changes, *Parash Pathar* was seen by most of the audience as a satiric comedy. It is also a socio-political document based on real-life incidents of significant importance. With sudden affluence, Paresh Babu has dreams of making it big in the political scenario, to be included in the inner circle of 'high society' people with their drinking parties. But Paresh Babu finds that he does not quite fit into this changed scenario. The affluent, Westernised Bengali snobs refuse to accept him in their fold and snub him openly, taking potshots at his humble roots and lifestyle.

As Paresh Chandra Dutta passes Raj Bhavan, thunder showers begin unexpectedly and his torn umbrella cannot protect him. So he steps into Curzon Park and takes shelter under a column constructed by the British. He suddenly sees a stone rolling towards him in the rain water. He is yawning and very drowsy, and whether he actually sees the stone is not clear at this juncture. The next shot shows a rain-drenched Paresh Babu walk through a narrow alley towards his home.

It is later discovered that Paresh Babu has brought home the stone which has the magic power to turn everything it touches to gold. Until the end of the film, one is kept wondering whether his experience was derived from real life or whether it was his imagination playing tricks, or a dream.

As he demonstrates the stone's magical power to his wife by changing a few household items into gold, Ray uses his inventiveness with irony by showing a metallic statuette of a British soldier Paresh Babu turns into gold. This is a metaphor for the British, who once ruled India but have now been reduced to a tiny toy soldier that can be turned into gold with the touch of an Indian's magic stone.

Soon, the Duttas are among the richest citizens of Calcutta. From a modest dwelling, the childless couple moves to an opulent mansion. Paresh now has a personal secretary Priyatosh Henry Biswas, a young man preoccupied with his girlfriend. The source of Paresh's sudden wealth is a mystery and Paresh is very careful to keep it a secret. He is now much sought after in social and political gatherings.

There is one comical scene where Paresh Babu is looking at a statue. As the camera zooms into the statue, we find that the head is that of Paresh Babu himself, smiling and nodding his head as if in acknowledgement of an invisible crowd looking up at him! This is one of the most ironic scenes in the film.

The bank clerk's discovery has a larger impact on the price of gold in the market. The price of gold begins to fall drastically, creating panic in the bullion market. People begin to sell off their gold in a tearing hurry. One scene shows a very poor woman digging the gold she has hidden in a hole in the ground only to find that it has turned into stone. No one knows what hit them.

The lucky couple's happiness is short-lived, though. His

suave secretary swallows the magic stone which dissolves in his stomach. Peace and harmony return to the very confused and disturbed Paresh Babu's life. He heaves a sigh of relief. This is a departure from Parasuram's original story where Paresh Babu is very sad when the magic stone disappears.

The magic stone in *Parash Pathar* is like a toy in the hands of Paresh Babu's neighbour's son to whom he initially gives the stone in exchange for a nonsense rhyme he wishes to hear him recite. Later, he bribes the stone back from the boy, swapping it for sweets.

There is a sweet scene of camaraderie between Paresh Babu and his wife. He runs after her with a gold chain round and round the old four-poster bed; feeling shy, his middle-aged wife tries to escape him in their very humble living space. It is an example of the contented life the childless Paresh Babu led with his wife, which changes with his dismissal from his job and the arrival of the stone.

From a mere toy in the beginning, the stone becomes a concrete object of acquiring physical wealth. It leads to

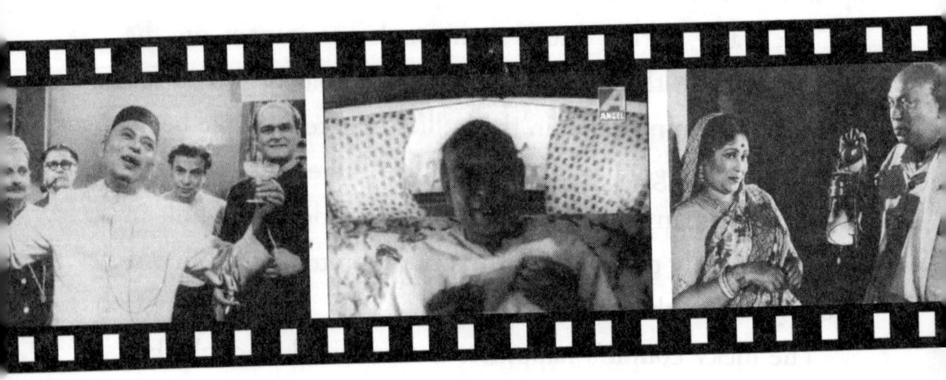

dangerous repercussions in the economy yet it is an agency for social upliftment, a window to political and social aspirations and finally, an instrument that makes Paresh Babu distinctly uncomfortable and unhappy over time. Finally, it disappears from Paresh Babu's life as suddenly as it appeared.

Interestingly, the appearance of the magic stone does not change the richness of Paresh Babu's character. He does not misuse the immense power he has as owner of the stone. His wish-fulfillment is simple—own a car, start a business, shift to a spacious home and run an ordinary office with a stylish secretary. He demonstrates the secret of the magic stone at a 'high-society' cocktail party when he gets drunk for the first time in his life, because he finds the elite invitees laughing at him and slighting him.

The cocktail party scene plays a dramatic role in the film in several ways. First, it features some of the most famous stars in Bengali cinema of the time, featuring in guest appearances, perhaps because it is a Ray film. Second, it reveals the face of Bengali society where social acceptance is entirely dependent on how rich you are and how you can show off your affluence, hold your liquor, speak English and join in ballroom dancing, none of which Paresh Babu can do.

On their part, the guests are taken aback with this very ordinary middle-aged man, wondering how he has become affluent enough to have been invited to this party. They judge him by his simplicity, his inability to hold his liquor and his failure to socialise with this new crowd, the likes of which he has never met in his life. Paresh Babu, perhaps in anger and perhaps to show off, gets dead drunk and spills the secret of his wealth to a rich Marwari businessman who offers to buy the stone at any price. But Paresh Babu is not a greedy man. He does not bend.

The magic stone's relationship with Paresh Babu has much more meaning than what is apparent at first glance. Its physical presence is only one aspect of its existence. It makes the film a political statement, a social critique on class distinctions, a science fantasy, a social satire and a futuristic prophecy. The stone has multiple utilities. For the boy, it is a toy. For Paresh Babu, it creates a new lifestyle and a new image, opening a door to the tantalising possibility of social elevation. For Biswas, it is an instrument to commit suicide when his girlfriend ditches him. For the Marwari businessman, it has the use-value of gaining infinite wealth that will lead to greater power to exploit the situation by abusing the power of the stone and oppressing the masses. Yet it is so fragile that it can be ingested by an ordinary young man.

Thus the stone symbolises different things for different people at different times and phases within the film. The Marwari businessman tries to blackmail Paresh Babu to part with his 'formula' for the magic stone. Paresh Babu uses the same nonsense rhyme as the 'formula' for this businessman with evil intentions. The nonsense rhyme has two different use-values and sign-values in the film that also has direct links with the magic stone and Paresh Babu. It has sign-value within a system of objects in the time-place-social setting it is placed in.

Conclusion

In *Parash Pathar*, values do not just exist, values are also created along the way. Other objects come into the picture: (a) X-ray plates (b) the metal soldier—the first object that turns into gold that could have the political interpretation of a joke on the recently ended British rule in India (c) Paresh Babu's second hand car (d) his wife's gold chain the husband-wife pair have a sweet game with (e) Paresh Babu switching over from smoking bidis to cigarettes (f) Paresh Babu's first encounter with alcohol and so on. In this sense, the magic stone functions as a 'creator' of other objects that evolve different kinds of relationships not only with Paresh Babu but also with his wife and his secretary.

Many critics have felt that *Parash Pathar* is perhaps Ray's best film. It is a socio-political comment, a comedy, a satire and also, has elements of black comedy. But above all this, it deals with a universal theme that is timeless and holds true in all cultures at all times. It was made in 1958 but holds meaning more than sixty years after it was released.

PRATIDWANDI WHO IS THE ADVERSARY?

Pratidwandi (The Adversary) is said to be the first among the three city-centred films Satyajit Ray decided to make. This celluloid journey that began in 1970 was followed by *Seemabaddha* (1971) and ended with *Jana Aranya* (1973) to peel off, layer by layer, like the skins of an onion, the psyche of youth in an ever-changing Kolkata.

The feature that makes the trilogy memorable is the common thread of turbulence in the city, both in physical, social and environmental terms that critiques the corrupt ethos of corporate firms, and more importantly, the inner struggle it creates within the psyche of the protagonist on the one hand and the conflicts—sometimes real, sometimes imaginary—these create to push the story forward.

All three films were celluloid adaptations of novels authored by two famous Bengali authors: Sunil Gangopadhyay wrote *Pratidwandi* while *Seemabadha* and *Jana Aranya* were authored by Sankar. But Ray improvised on the original stories according to his own contemporary demands as a scriptwriter and director.

About Ray toying with Gangopapdhyay's original literary work, film scholar and author Suranjan Ganguly writes:[6]

> In his adaptation of Sunil Gangopadhyay's *Pratidwandi* (The Adversary, 1970), Satyajit Ray upholds the right of the filmmaker to deviate from the original and create an autonomous text, which retains its link to its source

> but is also an interpretation in its own right. Through a series of "excavations," he unearths ideas and issues that circulate in the novel but often remain understated or underdeveloped—some mere allusions, others key events which acquire a different frame of emphasis in his film. These excavations enable him to make certain conceptual changes that allow for another text—as it were—to emerge, one which lies submerged within the book.

The protagonist in *Pratidwandi*, Siddhartha Choudhury, is forced to give up his medical education when his father dies suddenly and he has to join the swarms of educated, middle-class young men looking for employment. Failing to get a job despite being competent and educated, he takes to walking on the city's streets or wandering across to the digs of his two classmates from medical school and ruminating on how he can stop his younger brother from engaging in dangerous Naxalite activism or his sister from engaging in an affair with her boss.

However, even his efforts on the personal front prove

infructuous because his brother Tunu shrugs him off while his sister, Sutapa, a very attractive young girl, reminds him that after their father's death, she is the sole income earner in the family. Siddhartha suspects that she is being sexually pressurised by her boss but being the escapist that he is, he does not do anything about it. The director suggests that the sister is preparing herself for a career in modelling.

This was a turbulent time in many parts of India, in West Bengal, in general and Calcutta, in particular. Frustration arising from poverty, unemployment and social inequalities led young men like Siddhartha's brother to involve themselves in active and violent resistance, exploding at times into violence against all forms of authority. On one hand, the state of West Bengal and its capital city was the epicentre of much of this 'revolutionary thinking'. On the other hand, the public and private sector were building up a culture of bribes and corruption, with the older generation teaching the youngsters how to 'get ahead in life'.

With issues like rising unemployment, the rise of the underground Naxalite movement appropriated a slew of brilliant students of Calcutta and Jadavpur Universities within its fold, committed to uproot capitalist and/or fascist rule through armed revolution. Alongside, there was an influx of hippies from the West, white-skinned youngsters from the US and European places living a Bohemian life, doing drugs, dancing away on the streets of Calcutta, enamoured with the poverty, the dirt and the debris. In one indoor scene, we find one hippie trying to hear the sound of a *khanjani* (a percussion instrument used mainly in religious songs) through a stethoscope! It is a fleeting scene but carries its own comment.

Is Siddhartha a coward or an escapist? Or is he a misfit? He is really a microcosm of the city's youth who want to be upwardly mobile and yet are not ready to compromise on the moral values they have imbibed to fit into the fast-changing corporate world. His cowardice comes across when he suddenly, on an impulse, visits his sister's boss at his residence but walks away without 'shooting him down' though that was his original plan. His escapism comes across in many ways, especially when he refuses to work for a political party even for a salary. That he is a misfit, we learn from his complete distancing from his family, especially his constantly weeping mother. He shows concern for his kin but is clearly not involved at all.

In *Pratidwandi*, the opening scene is presented in a negative print, to highlight how the death of the protagonist Siddhartha's father has turned his world inside out and upside down. Later, an encounter with a trained and uniformed nurse moonlighting as a sex worker is presented in the same way, again giving us a sense of how deeply unsettling this moment is to Siddhartha. When he is about to cross a main street, he sees a young, buxom woman trying to cross the same street from the other side and his mind switches back to his medical class with the professor explaining the anatomical details of a woman's breast. Once visiting the home of a pretty young girl who becomes his girlfriend of sorts, when the girl's would-be stepmother tries to swallow a pill for her headache, Siddhartha once again breaks up that image into a negative print. These seem to suggest that he has not been able to forget that he was forced to leave his medical education for a job but ironically, fails to land that job.

He dreams a lot but his dreams are more nightmares than dreams. He goes to watch a movie where the airconditioned cool on a summer afternoon is ideal for an afternoon nap and not the movie itself. We once see him go with a friend to watch a Swedish film at a film club which, the friend points out, has "no cut." But the film turns out to be a joke on what they were looking for—uncensored sex scenes in the film. In another nightmare, Siddhartha sees his sister in a bathing suit posing for photographs on a beach. The picture changes to Tunu being gunned down by a firing squad. A nurse comes to tend to him but when she looks up, it is his sister Sutapa whose face melts to become Keya's face. All this happens on an empty beach with the tide ebbing and flowing in. Ray visualises this scene as if bringing it out of reality and placing it neatly within a surreal world from Siddhartha's point of view.

His younger brother Tunu takes pot-shots at him labelling

him a conformist and a coward, pointing out that this same older brother had bought him a thick biography of Che Guevara; Siddhartha smiles wistfully to remind him that he had to sell off two thick medical books to buy this one for Tunu's birthday. If the medical books have lost their use for Siddhartha, Guevara's life too, now seems to have become an exercise in futility.

He accidentally gets into a brief relationship with Keya, a sweet young college girl who suffers from feelings of loneliness and a sense of rejection because her father is about to marry her aunt, who constantly tries to draw attention to herself. Though Siddhartha goes on a few dates with Keya, his body language, his silences, his brief conversations with her do not give the impression that he is ready to take the relationship seriously.

In fact, Siddhartha has no idea about what direction his life is taking which, perhaps, is a reflection of Calcutta itself, where hippies wander about aimlessly beside an unemployed young man, a well-spoken nurse moonlights as a prostitute, a medical student from an affluent family has no issues pocketing the money someone has collected for charity. We get a glimpse of a time when candidates have no proper place to sit for an interview and they must wait the whole day for a meeting that lasts for hardly five minutes. The walls of the hall where the candidates are waiting are filled with political graffiti and we learn that the office is shifting to another place.

The only evidence of Siddhartha's rootedness lies in his search for that unique birdcall he heard as a child. He goes in search of it at New Market but he does not know the name of the bird so the search is in vain. That birdcall keeps haunting him at odd times and we feel that this is his escape back to his boyhood days, a sweet memory trapped in his consciousness forever.

Siddhartha is fleshed out as an introvert, an 'outsider' who sees things through the lens of his medical lectures, in the negative. He finds it almost impossible to agree with his panel of interviewers who have decided that he has communist political leanings because he prioritises the Vietnam war over man's landing on the moon. He imagines the worst when his sister comes home very late, only to discover later that she is attending modelling classes. But he remains suspicious though he lacks the nerve to confront her face to face.

The camera wanders across the city, sometimes casually, sometimes idly, sometimes rapidly following Siddhartha's tracks, scanning the public vehicles we see Siddhartha jostling in with the huge crowd, hanging from the slings, squeezing himself in and out of the overcrowded entrance without making even an acquaintance.

The sights and sounds the camera and the sound design capture are often from Siddhartha's point of view while in other scenes, they make Siddhartha the subject of their focus and the audience enjoys both points of view, giving it a chance to draw its own conclusions when Siddhartha leaves Calcutta to go to a district to work as a medical salesman.

Towards the end, at a very crowded interview waiting room with just one functioning fan and seventy-five candidates waiting in the sweltering heat, we find Siddhartha angry for the first time in the entire film. He dashes into the room where the interviewers are seated and tried to explain the need of proper seating for the candidates waiting outside. He is asked to wait. When he comes out and joins the crowd, he suddenly visualises the waiting candidates reduced to skeletons of themselves, with a dry, authoritative voice-over narrating in English the significance of parts of a human skeleton. He emerges from his trance to find the candidates back in their human form. This is the only time we find Siddhartha, normally a very quiet young man, bursting out in anger. His anger is directed not so much on those suited-booted corporate honchos but at the entire socio-economic system that has effectively reduced one huge mass of humanity to waiting skeletons of themselves and another smaller group fighting to keep them trapped in the skeleton image.

Dulal Dutta's brilliant editing follows Siddhartha striding out of the hall with angry steps after crashing into the interviewing room, overturning the table, bashing up whoever tries to come in his way, walking out, the graffiti on the walls speeding along with the speeding Siddhartha till suddenly we have a look out of a speeding train, at the raised hand of Siddhartha with a cigarette, moving away from Calcutta to take up the job of a medical salesman in Balurghat he had earlier decided against accepting.

He gets into a seedy hotel and while penning a letter to Keya, he suddenly hears that bird-cry in the midst of the chanting of *Bolo Hori Hori Bol* (A chant sung when dead bodies are carried to the crematorium) as in long shot, a body is being carried to the crematorium. He walks up to the balcony and signs off the letter to Keya. The sound of the chant of pall-bearers mixing into the sweet, whistling cry of that bird Siddhartha had been searching, signs the full circle of life and death.

Who is the adversary here? Is it the city of Calcutta that is slowly moving towards a shift in values that seems to be working against the youth, be it Tunu who is drawn into an extremist movement that believes in the use of arms to quell the establishment? Or, is it Siddhartha's sister, Sutapa, who as the single earner of the family, appears to be willing to compromise with conventional values of morality to go up in life and become a model? Perhaps, it is Siddhartha himself who finds himself a misfit in the corporate world? Is the birdcall an entreaty to return to an innocent childhood when he is getting ready to face the world? As he loses the birdcall along the way, he also loses his space in the world he ought to have fitted himself into. These questions keep you guessing long after the film is over.

This film, through the eyes of its protagonist, shows us the slow but sure socio-political changes happening in Kolkata where interviews are fixed, where hippy youngsters dance in merriment, where unemployment among the educated young keeps climbing every day and yet, where a young man, defeated in the battle of life, seeks and finds succour in a simple birdcall lost in childhood.

NAYAK SLICE OF A HERO'S LIFE

Life is a journey, a process of travelling through time, space, experience and relationships. It is an ongoing process that begins with life and moves beyond death because even if the physical journey ends, memories are left behind for the people one is close to and the places in which one has lived and loved and worked during different phases of one's life. Cinema is at once a slice of life, a reflection of life, a window to life, a way of looking inwards into oneself and all these put together. Therefore, cinema also is a journey in itself. Within its genres of comedy, family drama, suspense, thriller, tragic love story, romance, there are road films and journey films that overlap these genres and, at the same time, are a genre in themselves in different ways.

Satyajit Ray's *Nayak* (The Hero), was one of four digitally restored Ray movies that was screened in PVR cinemas in January 2014. *Nayak* is comparatively sidelined among Ray's oeuvre but becomes a delightful rediscovery for one who has already watched the film before. Though it is an outstanding film, it seems to have been ignored by critics and film scholars compared to the attention paid to his other films. Some suspect that the reason is Ray's choice of Uttam Kumar, the *numero uno* of Bengali cinema of the time, to play the protagonist—who also happens to be a top star of Bengali cinema during the period in which the film is set. Uttam Kumar was a star, true. But he was also one of the most brilliant actors Bengali cinema has produced till date. The film is one of only three feature films in Ray's body of work that are not adaptations, and are original screenplays written by Ray himself.

Uttam Kumar was apprehensive about Satyajit Ray presenting him in *Nayak* without make-up. He had never done that before. In mid-1965, when shooting for *Nayak* began, Uttam Kumar had just recovered from a bout of chicken pox. Ray asked him to touch up his face only in the flashback scenes as a younger man. When shooting was over, Uttam Kumar said, 'I have discovered a new side to myself. Unhindered by make-up, I felt freer while expressing my emotions'.

Talking about his experience of having worked with Uttam Kumar, Satyajit Ray said, 'It turned out to be the most pleasant experience of my career. I found that he belonged to the breed of instinctive actors. I hardly recall any discussion with Uttam on any serious, analytical level on the character he was playing. He surprised and delighted me with unexpected little details of action and behaviour, which came from him and not from me, always in character and always enhancing a scene. They

were so spontaneous that it seemed he produced them out of his sleeve. If there was any cognition involved, he never spoke about it.' It looked like an autobiographical performance of a struggling actor who rises to the top, gets the National Award, but finds himself completely alone, distanced from his friends and peers, misunderstood by everyone.

The storyline spans the time it takes for Rajdhani Express to travel from Kolkata to New Delhi. Almost the entire film is shot inside the compartment of a moving train but in actuality, is a classic example of art director Bansi Chandragupta's magic creative powers. His design of the interior of a train for *Nayak* including the corridor, the dining car and even the toilet were so flawless that viewers took it to be real. It was not a real train at all while a real train speeding along the tracks created the pace for the film.

The story revolves around Arindam Mukherjee, the film-star hero, an icon who is travelling to Delhi to receive the National Award. His secretary, once his close friend, has failed to get a flight booking. Mukherjee is forced to get into the Rajdhani Express. Irritated with the unwanted attention of fellow-commuters, he shifts to the dining car. He chances upon Aditi Sengupta, the editor of a woman's magazine who is going to Delhi to get a grant for her publication. The physical and geographical journey changes into a journey of introspection for the hero and of discovery for the journalist.

Says Dipankar De Sarkar in his re-reading of the film:

> According to Ray, through *Nayak,* he wanted to 1. Investigate the psychology of a movie star; 2. Investigate

> the psychology of fans; 3. Make a film about a train journey. But there's one element in the critical narrative about Nayak that remains underplayed, and that is the character played by Tagore.[7]

The film opens on a close-up of the hero Arindam's head from the back showing him combing his hair after having shaved himself with an electric razor, a luxury only the rich could afford during the time the film is set in. As he readies himself to catch the Rajdhani Express, he converses with an old friend of his who is now his manager and confesses that he is a 'satellite' who cannot drink inexpensive tea. Arindam asks after the box office takings of his new film and the friend says that since this is the end of the month, and the film is just into its second week, it will take some time to pick up the takings. These scenes build up the character of a famous actor who lives alone, is arrogant to a fault and can also be rude when he feels like it.

The media runs like a strong undercurrent just beneath the main story. In the compartment, one of the coupes is occupied by a very old and very rigid-minded man named Aghore Chatterjee, who is known for his regular letters to the editor in *The Statesman*. Arindam steps into his coupe to have some fun at his expense when he is asked if he drinks, is married and so on. Arindam is haunted by the news report of his drunken scene two nights before at a party, a topic of gossip among other travellers in the train. Aditi Sengupta edits a woman's magazine named *Adhunika* (Modern Woman) but avoids using articles on films. The magazine does not have enough circulation so we find her requesting a subscription from one of the commuters she befriends.

Arindam agrees to give her an interview, which becomes an unfolding of his own life story, narrated to a perfect stranger he somehow gets to like—mainly because she treats him normally regardless of the aura he exudes. But the interview when Arindam is fully drunk causes him to regret his outpourings. To respect their brief bonding, and his regret for having given away his closely guarded secrets in a moment of drunken weakness, Aditi tears up the sheets in which she took notes during the impromptu 'interview', a prized assignment for her, in his presence. When Arindam asks if she will forget what she wrote, she smiles shyly and says, 'Will keep it in my heart,' an ambiguous statement.

There is an interesting anecdote Arindam unfolds from his past which bears a striking resemblance to a real-life experience of Uttam Kumar. An old friend of Arindam approaches him once and requests him to come along to a meeting. Arindam agrees after some hesitancy. But when he reaches the scene, he is terrified to find that it is a political meeting that may spoil his image as a top hero. Film stars in Calcutta in those days were not expected to be involved in any kind of political activity. He reverses the car to turn back, despite the persuasion of this friend but the memory remains archived in the recesses of his mind.

The real-life analogy comes from a true incident Uttam Kumar was reportedly witness to when he went for his morning walk in the Maidan. In 1971, Saroj Dutta (born

1914), communist revolutionary, fiery journalist-editor and poet, disappeared from the city. His was a copybook case of forced disappearance amidst widespread state repression on communist rebels. A secret killing that since became part of the urban folklore, a crime the state denies till date. His body was never found and the rumour went that Uttam Kumar had witnessed his killing or his abduction. The star was so scared that he ran away from the city and hid in Bombay (now Mumbai) with various relatives and came back only after the furore over the missing revolutionary died down.

Back to the film. When the train chugs into Delhi railway station, people and fans that have come to welcome the hero with huge floral bouquets and garlands surround him and soon a crowd takes shape. The journalist walks away quietly with her uncle. The hero tries to reach out and look at her over the heads of the crowd, but she does not turn back. For the journalist, it is just a chance but memorable encounter. For the hero, it is a painful emotional journey he had never bargained for. There is a real journey in a real train moving from Kolkata to Delhi. But the journey is multi-layered with different stories branching out of the central encounter between the famous hero and the obscure editor. There is also an inner journey Arindam embarks on through the flashback into his life during the interview he gives to Aditi, walking her through his evolution from a suburban theatre actor to a matinee idol. The physical journey marks a movement forward. The inner journey moves backwards into Arindam's narration into his past life.

The journey is filled with flashbacks that include a couple of nightmarish scenes from the hero's perspective. His character has a history that maps his journey as a small-town guy who used club theatre as a way to become a hero in films. But we do not learn about his family background—his parents, et cetra because in retrospect, these do not seem mandatory to the film. There are several journeys-within-the-journey in Rajdhani Express. Aditi is not given any history except what comes across during her talk. We learn that she is single, has a cousin and edits a woman's magazine. She is familiar with the name and face of Mukherjee but has hardly watched his films.

Ray was a master in choreographing and composing dream sequences ideally suited to the character. The first dream sequence shows Arindam walking across a mound of currency notes till he is sucked into a hole that opens within that sea of notes and drowns because his theatre mentor, Shankar-da, who died during the Durga Pooja immersion, firmly opposed Arindam stepping into films, stands in full make-up and costume and watches him drowning under the ocean of currency notes but does not stretch out his arm to pull him out.

The soundtrack is filled with the ringing of many telephones that spring up like mushrooms in that ocean of currency notes, held by skeletal hands and then, Arindam suddenly wakes up in a sweat.

The second dream is also a very dark and scary scene. Arindam is walking through a thinly treed forest and foliage when a female voice calls him from somewhere behind the bushes. It is a kind of hide-and-seek game which amuses Arindam in the beginning but he becomes intrigued by it as he cannot see the girl. 'For Arindam, a hoarding for one of his films exists in a dreamscape he wants to flee. Does he not like who he is in the films or who he's become because of them, or perhaps he fears being locked forever into that kind of image?' writes Beth Watkins in her comparative study of *Nayak* and *A Hard Day's Night* (1964) on the Beatles in *Silhouette* (May 2, 2015). The camera cuts to a dinner party where every guest is wearing dark glasses and looking back at him in complete silence when he enters the party. Someone tries to bash up Arindam. The scene then jumps to some anonymous railway station with the sound track filled with announcements over loudspeakers.

This is perhaps traced to the morning's newspaper reporting Arindam, in a drunken state, bashing up a man whose wife he is reportedly having an affair with. This links up to his real experience of a young and attractive woman suddenly coming to his home in the dark of the night and asking him to replace the fixed actress playing the heroine in *Moner Manush* with her. She looks extremely confident and smart and though Arindam shows her the door, in the dream, we see a huge hoarding of *Moner Manush* with large-size, crudely painted figures of Arindam and this pretty lady cast as his heroine.

These very dark, depressing and defeatist dreams reflect the pathos and the loneliness of Arindam with much greater intensity and depth than the other scenes in which he is awake. None other than Uttam Kumar could have gone under the skin and flesh and blood of Arindam Mukherjee the way he did. Sharmila Tagore as the journalist-editor Aditi Sengupta comes across with a low-key, subdued performance filled with restraint. There is one point when near the door of the compartment, she arrives to find Arindam completely drunk. At one point, in the dining car, Aditi takes off her glasses and Arindam, a bit surprised, tells her, 'Why, you look really good without your glasses' and she shyly looks down and does not respond.

The social markers are evident. Aditi is travelling in the chair-car of the train while the star is settled in a first-class coupe. The dining car that everyone has access to is the common denominator. The 'interview' becomes a kind of a 'confession' charting the slow and steady rise of Arindam Mukherjee to become the top star in the Bengali film industry with the usual quota of gossip in the media about his affairs with women, particularly one young woman who is married and visits him at his home one night trying to seduce him into giving her a role in films.

Nayak is a multi-layered film though on the surface, it appears to narrate the biographical history of Bengali cinema's top hero framed within a straightforward train journey, atypical of a matinee idol who would generally take a flight. The train journey is the framework, the backdrop and the centre stage within which Ray placed several stories, each featuring Arindam Mukherjee as the central figure. There is the 'social' journey the hero unwittingly embarks on as he is forced to interact with his fellow passengers in the same first-class coupe—a married couple and their teenaged daughter who appears to be frail and sickly. After a point, both mother and the teenaged daughter are equally besotted by the hero.

The mother (Bharati Devi) looks into her hand mirror to touch up her face. Another woman is married to a much older man. He is a marketing person who has no compunctions about using his wife to bag an assignment from an old, powerful would-be client travelling in the same train. But the wife refuses and the old man, an arrogant snob who bends backwards in praise of foreign films, angrily turns away. The same wife approaches Arindam in the corridor, asking him to help her get into films which Arindam diplomatically shrugs off. He has trained himself not to get rattled by the incessant stares of onlookers.

Behind the veneer of glamour, fame and star charisma, the narrative reveals that Arindam is a lonely, vulnerable and insecure young man with normal weaknesses and strengths like any other man of the street. During the journey, he tries to refrain from his usual addiction to cigarette and liquor as a courtesy to his fellow passengers but after some time, he smokes and drinks openly and even teases the old man Aghore

Chatterjee in a neighbouring coupe who keeps saying he cannot stand the smell of alcohol. He also suffers from pangs of guilt for having backed out of the promise he made to his theatre mentor, Sankarda, of not getting into films. The famous character actor who insulted him in front of the entire crew when Arindam was fresh and doing his first film, comes to the young actor's lavish home, beaten, poor, old and out of work, for whisky. This is a powerful comment on the impermanence of fame, glamour and affluence in the film industry.

Once they recognise him, passengers from other coupes and coaches approach him with different aims in mind, visibly awestruck with the rare opportunity of meeting Bengali cinema's top star in flesh and blood. The 'introspective' journey begins when Aditi approaches his table in the dining car requesting an autograph for her niece. He likes her because she is the only one among his co-passengers not awestruck by his starry glamour. There are the emotionally disturbing journeys through his nightmares. Most importantly, he goes through the introspective journey back into his life as a young man who rose to the position he finds himself in now—famous, rich, powerful but alone, without friends, misunderstood by the media, by old friends who approach him only to exploit his stardom, and young women who befriend him to get some role in a film.

The imaginative soundtrack with a single theme is exquisitely designed to fit into the running train ambience which changes from Arindam's first class coupe to the dining car where the sound of the wheels becomes very loud inside the toilet and louder when Arindam stands at the open door of the compartment and stares at the parallel tracks, possibly with thoughts of suicide flashing momentarily as the camera cuts back and forth to show the disturbed and sad expression on his face. *Nayak* may not have turned out to be so outstanding and brilliant had Ray not worked out such a wonderful casting coup by featuring the real-life star to portray the celluloid star. Aditi discovers through her brief but deep interaction with him that this man who has millions of followers rushing to take his autograph is basically no less ordinary, lonely and defeated than these 'followers' which includes the other passengers travelling with him to the capital city.

Road movies sometimes reveal an absence of moral virtues either in the characters who hit the road, or morally upright characters who tend to get stripped of moral virtues somewhere along the way. The road peels off the masks of travelers to their bare essentials. This happens when men and women leave the comfort of their rooted lives to step out into the unknown and the unexplored. This does not always hold true for the Indian road movies but *Nayak* is a classic example.

SADGATI DALIT SENSIBILITIES

Nearly 75 years since India became 'independent', the negative and marginalised associations of so-called low-caste people including untouchables has not become a relic of the past. In fact, the word 'Dalit' has brought in more torture and humiliation to this oppressed class, proving the famous Shakespearean saying, 'What's in a name?' One of the main leaders who touched the delicate chord of Dalits by labelling them as Harijan was Mahatma Gandhi.

The word 'Harijan' is derived from two words 'Hari' meaning God and 'jan' meaning person or people. Unlike Ambedkar who came from the Dalit community himself, Gandhi belonged to the upper caste. These Dalits, considered to be the lowest in the hierarchy of caste, were untouchable and even today, in some villages, they are not permitted to draw water from wells earmarked for upper castes, cannot cook for them or touch their food and so on. They are mostly engaged in very low-class work such as manual scavenging and cleaning of manholes and drains, tasks in which upper class people will never engage even they have to starve.

The representation of the Dalit in Indian cinema was marginal in the early stages of Indian cinema. Their celluloid visibility may have increased in recent times but in most films, the Dalit characters have been given a token nod or used as a ticket to awards and festival screenings or, very cleverly, as a strategy to enrich the narrative of a film which offers a pan-

Indian portrayal of many communities in the nation. A classic example of this is in Ashutosh Gowarikar's *Lagaan*.

Aamir Khan, with his sharply diplomatic intelligence, who has learnt the fine art of turning commerce into a social message and a mainstream film into a relevant socio-political statement, gives a token nod to the Dalit in *Lagaan*. Bhuvan 'accidentally' discovers that this young man with his limp hand can spin the ball extremely well, thereby harping on how his disability is an asset and not a liability for the cricket team. So, very cleverly, Khan blends the 'disability' and the 'Dalit' tickets at one go! Very convenient if you add the Dalit's silence to this! Bhuvan (Aamir) includes him in his cricket team. This angers the other members who refuse to practice and participate with an untouchable but Bhuvan wins them over to the extent of praising him for 'opening their eyes'. Really!

The young man's name is Kachra, which means 'waste' or 'garbage' in colloquial Hindi, perhaps laying bare the truth of his identity and social status. S Anand points out that though Kachra seems pleased to be included in the mainstream, albeit only for the match, his 'voice' is never heard. He is almost dumb and takes his marginalisation for granted. Anand pertinently points out that 'he is never asked whether he would like to be included in such a game. It is not clear whether this Dalit, portrayed so pathetically, is even aware of why the game is being played'.[8] Anand further points out that in *Lagaan*, no other character is identified by his caste or the faith he belongs to except Kachra. Why? Because he is the ideal scapegoat to demonstrate Aamir Khan and Gowarikar's lip service to the Dalit? The triumph lies in that *Lagaan* was a massive commercial hit and we all were mesmerised right through the two hours and forty minutes of its screening time.

> In Indian cinema, the body of the Dalit–male and female– presents a stereotypical contrast to the body of upper caste Hindus, Muslims and Christians. Viewed as untouchables, male Dalits are depicted as physically untidy, emotionally weak, intellectually hollow and an object to be abhorred because of their apparently 'low' birth. However, the female body, particularly that of young Dalit women is represented as sexually attractive and desirable– thereby, an object to be used and subjugated by the upper caste. This has been the case, generally, in most films made in Indian languages. However, the treatment of the Dalit body has not been static, rather it kept changing according to the socio-political developments and Dalit identity discourse, also the treatment of the Dalit body differs according to the location–rural and urban–of the film.[9]

Hardly a single film exploring the Dalit issue or identity or class has brought forth the truth in the brutal statement Ambedkar made way back in 1945 when he said, 'To the untouchable, Hinduism is a veritable chamber of horrors.'[10] The word 'untouchable' sounds contradictory if not funny in a country that prides in calling itself the world's largest democracy where the rulers come to power through the public mandate via general elections. In India, according to the 2011 Census, the population of Dalits is 20.14 crore which forms 16.6 per cent of the total population of the country.

Prakash Jha's *Damul* (1985) is a very good example of an excellent representation of the pervasive attack on Dalits. It is one of the boldest films to seamlessly explore casteist and capitalist politics in some pockets of rural Bihar. The onslaughts on the oppressed come like a whiplash. An entire Harijan *basti* is *gheraoed* to stop the residents from casting their votes, subjecting them to the mandatory repayment of debts they had never taken, forcing them to steal cattle for the landlord who leaves them to die if and when caught, but not at his doorstep. The final blow comes when Sanjeevana, an innocent Harijan from the Dalit *basti,* is sentenced to be hanged to death because he turned wise to the landlord's wicked ways; he becomes an easy victim as he is Harijan, desperately poor and illiterate.

The muteness from birth of the Dalit servant (Sadhu Meher) in Shyam Benegal's *Ankur* can also be interpreted as metaphorical as he belongs to the Dalit caste and works in the farm of the upper caste village landlord. This Dalit man cannot express his anger even when he can understand that his wife is being sexually exploited (a) because she is a servant and the wife of another servant (b) is young and attractive (c) is a Dalit.

Swati Mehta in *Exploring Caste in Hindi Cinema*[11] points out:

> ...the majority of the stakes in the film industry is held by higher castes, their films portray a very elitist image and way of life. The culture and traditions shown in the films, for instance, are very Brahmanical. Or one can say the concept of class has taken over caste in popular cinema. For instance, in Karan Johar's films or in films made by Yash Chopra, one comes across titles like Raichand, Mehra, Melhotra, mainly high caste Punjabis who are rich businessmen. Their marriage ceremony is based on Brahminical tradition, with the priest given supreme importance. Lavish weddings and related ceremonies are another feature, which reflects the feudal nature of Indian society. The rich and flamboyance can be attributed to the same.

When asked, 'Who are the Dalits in India?' Bama Faustina Soosairaj, one of the pioneers of Dalit feminist literature from Tamil Nadu who has emerged as a prominent voice among the sub-continent's women said:[12]

> People who are discriminated against and socially excluded on account of their caste and who militantly oppose such a system of discrimination and dehumanisation are Dalits. It also includes people who are marginalised based on class and gender.

Few are aware of *Dalit Camera*, a voluntary organisation founded in 2011 which functions in two Indian states: Maharashtra and Madhya Pradesh. They began with an ordinary still camera with a rudimentary video recording facility. Now with kindred support from various quarters, they own four cameras. 'One could describe Dalit Camera (DC) as a team of volunteers. We take videos of protest, public meeting, discussion, talks and upload it on the Internet. Expenses are usually met by voluntary contribution,' says the website.

Munshi Premchand

Munshi Premchand is perhaps rightly acknowledged as the most outstanding litterateur within Hindi literature. Born on 31 July 1880, Premchand's real name was Dhanpat Rai Srivastav and he hailed from a very middle-class family in Varanasi. Filmmakers over the decades have been deeply inspired by Munshi Premchand's works, though none of his stories lend themselves to the glamour, chutzpah and romanticism that Indian cinema demands.

His life was tough because he was forever plagued by health issues and financial constraints. Among the notable films inspired by Premchand's works, the first three names that crop up are Mrinal Sen's *Oka Oorie Katha* based on his famous story *Kafan* and Satyajit Ray's two films *Shatranj Ke Khilari a*nd the telefilm *Sadgati.*

Premchand wrote the original story *Sadgati* in 1931. Ray made it into a 50-minute black-and-white film for Doordarshan in 1981. Looking back on the film forty years after it was made, it remains as universal, timeless and relevant as it was when it was first written and thereafter was made into a telefilm by Satyajit Ray himself. In the 1930s, when Premchand wrote his story, Dalits were in a state of mute submission.

But the germs of Dalithood were sown many years before Premchand wrote *Sadgati* (Deliverance). According to Tapan Basu:[13]

> 'Dalithood is a kind of life condition which characterises the exploitation, suppression and marginalisation of the lower castes by the social, economic, cultural and political domination of the upper caste Brahminical order' is the way Dr Babasaheb Ambedkar defined the word 'Dalit' long before we included it in our common lexicon.

Munshi Premchand quit his government job at a school when he joined Mahatma Gandhi's non-cooperation movement of 1921. Burdened by family responsibilities, he began a printing press called Sarasvati Press in Varanasi but that too, did not do well and his financial woes continued. So, he called it quits and left for Bombay to try his luck as a scriptwriter for films.

He got a job of scriptwriter with Ajanta Cinetone. His first project was to write the story and script for a film titled *Mill Mazdoor* based on the rights of the working class. It was about the son and daughter of a textile mill owner who leaves the mill to his two children. While the son exploits the workers, the sister takes the side of the exploited, underpaid and overworked labour and even incites them to rise against the owners to demand their rights. The brother is jailed while the sister reopens the mill with the support of the workers.

But the reaction of the Censor Board was quite unexpected. The Censor Board felt that against the backdrop of the Great Depression of 1929 that had created a sense of dissatisfaction and anger among the workers, this film could have a negative impact on management-labour relations. Bombay was already a hotbed of militant labour activity and a movement was on. Rumours were rife that the man behind the holding back of the film was no other than Byramjee Jeejeebhoy, a member of the Censor Board, who was also the president of the Mill Owners Association. Its release in Bombay was not permitted. Interestingly, Premchand had played a small cameo in this film.

Stopped from release in Bombay, *Mill Majdoor* was released in Lahore, Delhi and Lucknow but there too, it was soon banned because it incited striking workers in these cities too. One group of workers who were employed in Premchand's own press rebelled against unpaid salaries and Premchand's dreams of making it in the Bombay film industry were shattered. And he left films for good. He died in 1936 with those shattered dreams without learning the impact of his writing on his readers and filmmakers in India. This did not stop other filmmakers to be deeply inspired by his works to make films on some of his stories. Agreed that his stories did not have the celluloid frequency that Sarat Chandra Chatterjee enjoyed but that is perhaps because they were too challenging to be placed on celluloid.

Add to this Trilok Jetley's *Godaan* and you confront a tragedy that is an ongoing violation of human rights in India. This underlines that Premchand's expression of the raw reality of his time is universal and these truths are perhaps more relevant, prominent and abundant today than they were then.

Mrinal Sen's *Oka Oorie Katha* suggests just the opposite—how some Dalits can bring their own ruin and remain immune to the tragedy happening to the woman in the family. Sen was roundly criticised by Premchand scholars for not showing the famous drunken scene of the father-son with the alms they have collected to buy the shroud *(kafan)* for the young bride while the dead body of the heavily pregnant Nilamma lies forgotten, with flies and insects infesting the corpse's body. However, the point has been made.

Shatranj Ke Khilari is an acidic political comment that offers a brilliant example of the interpretations of those events. The film is a recreation of a short story by Munshi Premchand of the same title.

Dalits in *Sadgati* (1981)

The film foregrounds the persistence of the caste system and its varying manifestations in contemporary India. The initial story was written much before independence in 1931, while Satyajit Ray adapted it in 1981. This is a crucial point of reference. The film was released much after the official abolition of untouchability but remains relevant. Cinema buffs and scholars should reflect on whether untouchability continues to be a reality today. If so, what are the various forms it takes and what are the consequences of such a practice for social equality and justice? Caste-based discrimination and atrocities remain common occurrences in our country. The question that arises, then, is whether a law can actually remove a social evil such as caste hierarchy that has been embedded in our social system.

The 50-minute film shot in black-and-white featured Om Puri as Dukhi, Smita Patil as Jhuria, Mohan Agashe as the Brahmin priest and Geeta Kak as his wife. Being shot in black-and-white adds to the edginess of the tragedy and the drama that could easily be a story picked from real life. Om Puri's almost skeletal frame, bent body and almost complete silence when asked to do the very heavy chores, and the anger expressed through his striking of his blunt axe on that unrelenting block of wood under the blazing sun adds to the credibility of the story and the performance.

Sadgati, primarily made for Doordarshan based on a Premchand story, deals with a *chamar* couple Dukhi and Jhuria. Dukhi arrives at the village priest's home to consult him about his minor daughter Dhania's impending marriage. The priest, a Brahmin, makes him go through such grinding hard work on an empty stomach and under the blazing sun that Dukhi collapses and dies. But no one will touch Dukhi's dead body and the priest is forced to drag the body by drawing it with a rope tied to his feet.

In his brilliant review of the film, Bhaskar Chattopadhyay writes:

> While Premchand's story is a scathing account of the tragic lives of untouchables in this country, and of the

> horrors of superstition and blind submission to the self-proclaimed voices of God, Ray's handling of the subject lends a sense of failure and dejection to the entire affair—even when Dukhi is alive—as if it's all over, and as if nothing can be done to help the poor man. Even as Dukhi seethes in rage and directs his fury at the log instead of his oppressor, muttering expletives at the lifeless piece of wood, we can't help but accept that we have failed him, in all possible ways. We feel as if his mere existence, his entire life, all up to this point, has been a lie—that he was born a slave and that he would die a slave, never to question his master, never to stand up to him, or face him, or look him right in the eye to show that he resents him and everything that he stands for.[14]

Sadgati literary means 'deliverance' which means 'the state of being saved from a painful or bad experience'. This is an ironical statement considering the brutally inhuman way in which Dukhi dies suggesting his death was a kind of deliverance from the inhuman life he was conditioned to lead.

Dukhi, recovering from a fever, arrives at the home of Pandit Ghasiram, the village priest, to consult him about his girl-child's impending marriage. The priest makes him go through so much of grindingly hard work on an empty stomach and under the blazing sun that Dukhi collapses and dies. He has internalised his low status so deeply that it never occurs to him to explain his condition or raise his voice against such inhuman behaviour. When he is commanded to split a hard block of wood with a blunt axe under the raging sun, he wreaks his anger on the block of wood. When the wood finally splinters, Dukhi collapses and dies.

A fellow tanner serves as a witness to this event and urges the other tanners of the village to leave the body as it is, till the police arrive. The priest finds himself in a dilemma, as caste rules dictate that touching the untouchable Dukhi would lead to extreme pollution. When everyone refuses to remove the body due to the fear of police investigation, Ghasiram is forced to drag the body by tying a rope around the ankle to a faraway place. The body is left for scavengers to feed on.

Munshi Premchand, in his relatively short story, excels in portraying the shades of brutality of caste system and untouchability. The priest's exacting and cruel treatment leads to the untimely death of Dukhi but the priest does not care. He is more concerned about removing the dead body from the compound of his premises than the fact that Dukhi has died because of him. What Dukhi could not achieve in life he manages to do in death: Pandit Ghasiram, who considers the touch of Dukhi polluting, is forced to drag the dead body himself.

The priest is conditioned to internalise his power over people like Dukhi and his wife too, is a part of the system that 'normalises' her very rude behaviour towards Dukhi. Dukhi's wife Jhuria's cries and repeated knocks on the priest's door till she breaks down is one of the most touching scenes in the film. She knows that the priest will not face any punishment.

Another issue that the film touches upon is the educational divide: does it have to do with gender, or caste, or both? The daughter of the tanner is supposed to be married off at a very young age while the son of the priest has the privilege of getting educated.

It would be in the fitness of things to quote Shashwati Ghose who writes:[15]

> Through Ray's vision we are able to see the various images of the cruelty of caste system. From names (Dukhi: always in pain; Jhuria: wrinkles; Ghasiram: lord of grass) to food habits (when Jhuria wants to cook food for the priest and make him sit on their charpoy Dukhi rejects it saying it would lead to sacrilege as an untouchable can't cook food and offer to a Brahmin and no upper caste would touch the person or property of an untouchable) speaks of a caste-bound world.

Endnotes

1 His works include *Masculinities* (1995), *Masculinities and Globalisation* in *Men and Masculinities* Volume 1 (1998) and *The Men and the Boys* (2000).

2 *SubVersions,* Volume 1, Issue 1, (2013) 146-70.

3 Rupa, 2019, p.97.

4 *Exploitation, Victimhood and Performance: Interrogating Masculinity in Bariwali,* Rohit K Dasgupta, Tanmayee Bannerji, Film Quarterly, Volume 69, Issue 4, Summer 2016.

5 Much of the data and socio-historical background and details for this film is credited to the chapter on *Parash Pathar* in *Panchali Thekey Oscar Part I* jointly authored by Ujjal Chakraborty, Aniruddha Dhar and Atanu Chakrabarti, Pratibhas, 2010, pp. 81-110.

6 *Excavating the Text: Ray's Adaptation of Pratidwandi /The Adversary* in *South Asian Review*, 2015, Volume 36, Issue 1: 'Satyajit Ray'.

7 *Mint*, 3 December 2013.

8 'Eating With Our Fingers, Watching Hindi Cinema and Consuming Cricket', Siriyavan, *Outlook*, 14 May 2002.

9 Ibid.

10 Roy, Arundhati, 'India's Shame', December 2014, *Prospect* magazine.

11 *Meri News,* 4 April 2009.

12 Interview with Professor Jaideep Sarangi, *Muse India*, 2012b.

13 *Translating Caste,* 2002, Katha.

14 https://www.firstpost.com/entertainment/ 8 October 2017

15 Contemporary Relevance of Premchand's *Sadgati*: A Sociological Review of Satyajit Ray's Film. PhD Scholar, UGC-Junior Research Fellow, Department of Sociology, JMI.

FEMININITY IN RAY'S FILMS

THERE IS A KIND of monotony in the way women within the family are typecast in cinema as clichéd plastic models and to some extent in literature as well. Generally speaking, the two extremely polarised images of women we are familiar with are (1) the chaste, docile and submissive woman who is conditioned to martyr herself for any cause linked to the family and (2) the promiscuous, vile and voluptuous woman whose values are diametrically opposed to the values held sacrosanct by the former. The former is placed on a pedestal and celebrated while the latter is condemned and ostracised.

Sadly, the grey areas between these extremes of black and white do not seem to exist for the average filmmaker. Both categories of women can easily be reduced to the lowest common denominator of being stripped of choice, and of exploring spaces within which they can grow beyond the parameters within which the family rigidly fixes them. Most accusations of the perpetration of these clichéd celluloid images of womanhood and wifehood in cinema are directed at men, since they form the majority of filmmakers across the world in general and in India in particular.

None of Ray's women on celluloid can be reduced to clichés as they defy every imaginable kind of stereotyping. Nor do they permit getting ghettoised within the Ray films. For Ray, therefore, it is not a question of representing either real women, or women of fantasy or women from literature. It is rather, a question of filmic representations of women contributing to and constructing our understanding of what a woman is: of a re-thinking and re-conditioning of what we have been used to, through and by mainstream cinema. He has never attempted, in any way whatsoever, to define a non-patriarchal representation of women. But he has proved, time and again, in film after film, that though conventional narratives themselves are complicit in projecting women as subordinate, it is for the creative imagination of a director like himself to use these very forms to present positive, dynamic and alternative representations of women.

Ray belonged to a family that for two generations at least was influenced by English liberalism. But it may be noted that this in no way alienated them from the family's Bengali intellectual roots. Both Upendrakishore Ray Chowdhury and Sukumar Ray, Ray's grandfather and father, were deeply rooted in the soil of Bengal, its literature, music, politics, philosophy and culture. In other words, Ray's upbringing was marked by a fine amalgamation of the two cultures he imbibed and assimilated within his system almost unconsciously like a child learns his language by repeating words his mother uses to put him to sleep, or feed him while narrating stories.

Ray was born in 1921 when the masses were still reeling under the impact and the scars inflicted by World War I. Liberal humanism, a characteristic of nineteenth century Bengal, was going through a process of great change. A section of the intellectual Bengalis had shifted its values and ideologies to Marxism and more radical ideas. The Indian People's Theatre Association came into being during the days of World War II when Ray was a young man. IPTA used cultural performances of music, song and theatre to become a strong, Leftist, politico-ideological force, specially in Bengal, which gradually spread to the rest of India. Ray was never a direct participant in the movement created by IPTA. Nor was he actively involved in any of the Marxist ideologies or politically inspired cultural movements. Though he remained keenly aware of the changes sweeping across the Indian horizon, he was still steeped in Tagore and all that Tagore stood for. This does not mean that he was immune to the other movements. He preferred to remain a liberal humanist without subscribing to any political persuasion.

Before one gets into the complex issues of the way he presented, portrayed and interpreted women in his films, it is necessary to read briefly his background and location, his formative years, the colourful and gifted company in which he grew up and the conditions and circumstances that shaped and sharpened his intellect, his sensibility and his remarkable grasp over the arts.[1]

To quote Ray, 'I am interested in people, in human beings,

in human character, in their interplay in the relationship of characters. That fascinates me in itself.' This indicates quite clearly that Ray's commitment is to the human being that covers men, women and children that emerge from his choice of subjects, stories and plots of his versatile oeuvre. The humanism was inculcated within him through his intellectual and culturally rich background in general, his stay in Santiniketan and his mother's deep influence in particular. Ray's humanism is designed to be relevant and meaningful to the needs and aspiration of his own people. His mother okayed the choice of little Chandana Banerjee (Mukherjee) for the role of Ratan in *Postmaster*. She taught Kanika Majumdar the entire Tagore song *Baaje Koruno Shurey* minus the support of percussion just so that she could lip-sync the song correctly while filming for *Monihara*, the second story in the Tagore trilogy, *Teen Kanya*.

Pather Panchali was released soon after Independence because it took a long time in the making. Every Indian was full of hope about being free Indians in a free country, free from the clutches of British rule at last. But hopes died before they could be articulated properly and promises were broken with impunity and without feeling. The Bengali middle class, that included Ray, was thoroughly disillusioned with the social realities of inequality, increasing poverty and rising unemployment among the educated middle class. 'Ray observed the play of political contradictions, social forces and economic interests during these troubled times with a depth and maturity that is not given to many. If the times were bad, the confusions and contradictions they bred in the middle class were even worse. And these found reflection in film after film by Ray.'[2] Ray stands out primarily as an artist of human concerns. Sad that this facet of his filmmaking has not got the attention it deserved.

Ray successfully structured his Charu, Arati, Bimala and Monisha out of dominant modes of representation. He never intended to structure any 'corrective' or any 're-ordering' of women characters in cinema. Nor did he resort to difficult and *avant gardist* strategies. All he had was to alter the language of cinema to suit his creatively challenging ends. He did this, by creating his own film language for, and of women. He did not compromise on aesthetic challenges to make his statements on women. He did not need to. He used his aesthetics to alter modes of female representation, and he did this without any expectation of making the box-office his final target.

Pather Panchali has given Indian cinema some women who are as classic as they are contemporary. We have the literary archetypes—the housewife Sarbajaya, the doddering old aunt, Indir Thakrun, the growing daughter Durga, and the young bride Aparna. Sarbajaya is throbbingly alive on screen, adding flesh and blood to the literary character Bibhutibhusan Bandopadhyay created with his gifted pen. Sarbajaya, Apu's mother, a semi-literate, naive, a bit rustic and poor, grows through *Pather Panchali* and *Aparajito* from a young mother to middle-age, from the epicenter of her family to woman impoverished more by her loneliness than by the poverty that dogs her all her adult life. Despite the humiliating poverty, she does her best to hide from her neighbours. Sarbajaya has a quiet dignity about her and still believes in the value of honesty. The anger that runs like an undercurrent is anger directed at the poverty she is trapped within and can do nothing about.[3]

Seemabadha throws up two sisters—Dolon, the acquiescent one, and Tutul, the one with a conscience. The elder sister Dolon has chosen the comfortable life of a senior executive's wife and she and her husband, Shyamalendu are this apparently nice couple who do not ultimately stand up to younger sister Tutul's scrutiny. Tutul sees the shallowness of the glitzy life and the price that one has to pay and it makes her cringe. She does not make a big hue and cry about it but in one quiet, firm gesture returns a watch that her brother-in-law had given her to wear. She takes a stand, reminding one of what Ray once remarked: 'I think I have perhaps a subconscious conviction about women—that they are basically more honest, more forthright—because physically they are the weaker sex, there are perhaps certain compensating factors in the general makeup of their characters.[4]

An upper-class, apparently liberated woman Aparna in *Aranyer Din Ratri* loses to the male hero Ashim during the course of a memory game because she knows that if she wins, it may kill her chances with him. Ray never gives in to the temptation of glorifying these characters, by making them feminist heroines as lesser filmmakers often do, thus putting political statement above the character's rootedness. Ray's loyalty is always to a truthful portrayal of characters, who ring true because they are rooted and because he understands them so well. Like Dayamoyee in *Devi,* who is a victim of her father-in-law's superstitions and a patriarchal, feudal set-up. Or Anila in *Agantuk*, who is human enough to be suspicious of the suddenly-surfaced uncle but also humane enough to not want to slight a man who might actually be her uncle.[5]

Ray's films looked at as a body of work of an *auteur* director, simultaneously depict a society where women are silenced, their experience and particular insights undermined and dismissed, and convincingly depict the legitimacy and coherence of women's position and experience. Yet, they are as different from each other as chalk from cheese. Arati of *Mahanagar* bears not the remotest resemblance to Charu of *Charulata,* though the same actress, Madhabi Mukherjee portrays both roles. Note, however, that men are not portrayed as the perpetrators of women's oppression. Though Ray himself confessed to having slowly switched over to themes of social relevance only in the last part of his career, his earlier 'literary' phase, where he explored classical writers like Bibhutibhusan (the *Apu* Trilogy) or Tarashankar (*Jalsaghar, Abhijaan*) or Parasuram (*Parash Pathar*) or Prabhat Kumar Mukhopadhyay (*Debi*) and of course, Tagore (*Charulata*, *Teen Kanya*, *Ghare Baire*), are no less socially relevant statements on life, fairness and justice to humanity. He may not have consciously designed them to be so. But as the films evolved into a final creative work of artistic expression, one discovered that they had simultaneously, perhaps unwittingly, evolved into strong social statements as well without any attempt at labelling or slogan raising. Two women from two of Ray's outstanding oeuvres, namely, *Charulata* and *Mahanagar*, might help confirm this belief.

DEVI THE HUMAN 'GODDESS'

Devi is based on a story by Prabhat Mukhopadhyay who built it on a concept created by Rabindranath Tagore. The story was published in 1899 in the *Bhadra* (July-August) issue of *Bharati*, a Bengali monthly magazine. Ray picked up the story to use it as his personal celluloid tirade against the mindset of the feudal Hindu Bengali who can stretch superstition far enough to 'sacrifice' an innocent young girl by deifying her as goddess Kali. The story is set in 1800 at Chandipur in rural Bengal. The original story (by Mukhopadhyay) had a different timeline. Ray's *Devi* is set in September-October of 1868, almost seven decades later.[6]

Dayamoyee and her husband Umaprasad live with his elder brother Tarapada, his wife and wealthy father, Kalikinkar Roy, a deeply religious person whose life revolves around his devotion to Goddess Kali. He spends his entire time worshipping Kali installed in a small temple inside his spacious home. His older son Tarapada, his wife Harasundari and their little boy Khoka live with Kalikinkar. The younger son Umaprasad studies in Kolkata. The family presents the image of an extended, affluent Bengali family of that period. Then Kalikinkar has a dream that topples the balance that had kept the wheels of the Roy family rolling smoothly. Only apparently because we find that between the two daughters-in-law, Harasundari, the older one, is completely marginalised when compared with the prime space and importance accorded to the younger Dayamoyee. In that sense, does this not lead to questions around why Dayamoyee is so prioritised? Because she is very young, more beautiful—and being childless, more accessible and approachable than Harasundari?

One night, Kalikinkar dreams that Dayamoyee is actually an incarnation of the goddess Kali and she has come into his home in human form as reward for his unstinted devotion to the goddess. Next morning, a shocked, confused and terrified Dayamoyee is installed as a goddess on a raised platform of the mansion's outer home. What happens then—to Dayamoyee, to her relationship with Umaprasad, to Kalikinkar and to the other members of the family—completes this tragic tale of how blind belief in superstition can destroy the life of a young girl of seventeen. The credits rise across images showing the slow sculpting of the image of the goddess. The goddess stands out in all her finery of shimmering silver and gold *zardozi* decoration at the onset of Durga Puja. Drums and cymbals fill the soundtrack.

Devi depicts the classic example of a young girl turned into an icon—an object—by placing her on the pedestal of a goddess without her permission or understanding of what is happening to her and why, just on the basis of the dream of an elderly man. Turning the subject into an object of veneration, of beauty, of devotion and of blind faith is unique in Indian cinema that can be seen as entrapment for life for the young girl.

Does the old widower feel sexually attracted to the beautiful young daughter-in-law? If not, then why does he probe into her relationship with her husband, which, according to the traditional conventions he practices so diligently, he is not supposed to? Why does he allow her to press his feet, and be by his side the whole day till she is installed as the goddess? Why does he, under the 'excuse' of deifying his daughter-in-law, stop the very young couple from enjoying a normal conjugal life? These questions were unthinkable during the time setting of the story and they still are among Hindu fundamentalists who display ignorance about their own religion.

Feminist scholar Bishnupriya Ghosh propounds the same theory.[7] She writes:

> Dayamoyee is positioned as an object of desire for her father-in-law who cross-examines her closely, if teasingly, about her relations with her husband. Through his gazes, conversation and his demands on her time and labour we can see his erotic attachment to his young daughter-in-law, even though all this is played out within the norms of socially accepted behaviour within extended families.

Dayamoyee was content in her husband's open fondness for his teenaged wife. Just before Umaprasad leaves for Kolkata, we see him writing his name and address in English in his beautiful slanting hand on white envelopes for Daya to write to him 'everyday,' he says, smiling. He writes the address on fifty envelopes, 'one for each day' of his absence. But the envelopes remain unused because Daya gets trapped in her goddess mode where every waking minute is strictly monitored, designed and tailored by her father-in-law with the help of his servants.

Later, we find Harasundari fetching one of these envelopes to summon Umaprasad and rescue his wife from this torture. He does arrive but Daya, in deep doubt about the tussle between her human identity and her goddess one, refuses to go. The addressed envelopes that mark the adoring love of a husband for his wife become an exercise in futility due to the machinations of a third man—the husband's father.

Umaprasad could have pleaded to stop this autocracy of his father. He could have presented a strong defence to his family member or the villagers. But we do not see him doing any such thing. Nor does he speak of his problem with any among his family. His standing up to his father is weak and a failure. His family is much less educated so he knows that they will not look at his problem as he does and he will stick to convention. Therefore, he discusses the issue with his English professor. The professor, a Christian, analyses his problem but refrains from offering a solution.[8] For Umaprasad, it is truly a 'letting off of steam' and sharing his problem rather than finding a genuine solution. He is left with no option but calling his father 'insane' as he lacks the strength to take action.

An interesting contradiction in Umaprasad shows when he offers to talk to his friend's father about accepting the son's decision to marry a widow he is in love with. This friend tells him that his wealthy father will disinherit and disown him if he gets to know that the son wants to marry a widow. Then why does Umaprasad allow his wife to be sacrificed at the altar of religion instead of forcibly taking her away from such a toxic ambience to Calcutta? Through Uma's weak personality, Satyajit Ray presents a generation of intimidated young Bengalis.

Daya hardly talks once she is forced into the goddess mode. The steadily increasing stoop of her shoulders, the tired helplessness of her eyes, silent tears streaking down her cheeks, her reluctant acceptance of the shift from her bedroom to a room downstairs, say it all. The shift from private space where she has much more freedom to move and play with Khokon or talk to her parrot to the public space of the *thakurdalan*—the raised platform in the outhouse—traps her within a prison.

Women of nineteenth century Bengal, like women in other regions, were not economically or socially a homogenous group. Their lifestyles and occupations varied depending on whether they were from rich families, from the middle class were poor women. While women of rich families and middle stations stayed in seclusion in the *andarmahals* (or *antahpur*), the majority were working women, either traditionally self-employed like *naptenis*,[9] sweepers, vegetable vendors, fishmongers, maidservants, street singers and dancers and women employed by mercantile firms dealing in seed produce, mustard, linseed, etc. The poorer class of women used whatever time they had left after housework to assist the men in traditional occupations like cultivation, pottery, spinning, basket-making, etc. Such participation extended to cultural activities like community singing and dancing during festivals, as well as to *brata*[10] meant exclusively for women and performed with a view to attaining their aspirations as pious daughters, wives and mothers—mainly as mothers of male children. In other words, every *brata* practised by girls from a young age was designed for the welfare of others—sons and husbands—and not, repeat not, for their own welfare.

For their livelihood, poor working women had to move in the mainstream peopled by all kinds of men. This world was considered to be a dangerous society that was a threat to the sheltered sisters who lived in the *andarmahals* of upper-class Bengali families. For the members of the *andarmahal* or *antahpur*, these women were the only link to the world outside. With the decline of the village economy and the beginnings of industry in nineteenth century Bengal, there was a regular exodus of poorer men and women from the countryside to Calcutta.[11] So, because Kalikinkar was deeply convinced that Daya was really a human incarnation of Kali, he breaks these conventional practices of patriarchy and brought her out into the *bahir mahal*.

We never once see Daya eating. Does this mean that she is not fed properly? When she once faints of fatigue, it is interpreted as '*samadhi*' and she does not utter a single word.

She has absolutely no say in this shifting of space from the interiors of the mansion and though confused about this shift, does not ask or say anything. Her tender body is burdened by the weight of the garlands around her. One scene shows a serpentine queue moving in the far distance towards the Roy home to get a palmful of her *charanamrita*[12] (water from a vessel in which Daya's feet are dipped) which they believe has magical powers. Yet, we never find Kalikinkar trying to take commercial advantage of this sudden popularity of his home and his daughter-in-law. But the story belongs to a period when godmen and godwomen were created mainly for reasons of profit. Kalikinkar, though dictatorial and autocratic, was focused on Dayamoyee's magic powers.

Asked about her experience of playing the title role in Ray's *Devi*, Sharmila Tagore says:

> At that time, I was too little to actually understand the implications of the role I played in *Devi*. What helped was that I was very well-read even at that tender age. We were brought up within a culture of reading. There was no television, no computers or internet, and even movie-going was doctored and censored by the elders in the family...Dayamoyee, the character I played in the film, was around the same age as I was when I shot for it. I still remember that when the lights were being changed on the sets, I would often fall fast asleep on the huge four-poster bed. The crew would wake me up when the shot was ready. It ended very tragically for that young girl. The fact that the character and the

> one who played it—me—were the same age, helped, I think, because I did not have to pretend I was older than what I was.[13]

Sharmila went on to add that the film was widely misinterpreted in the West at the time. While everyone in Bengal is familiar with Kali worship and is aware of the nature of the orthodox family structure and its do's and dont's, the Western audience was not, and therefore experienced difficulty in following the course of events, as the development of the plot grows out of this orthodox Bengali nature of the theme.

> Even in India, there was a lot of trouble at the time of its release. The film became quite controversial as it was seen as an attack on Hinduism. The Communist government of the time also seemed unwilling to promote a film that talked of what they deemed was outmoded superstition. More so, because Ray was a Brahmo, it was hinted that he had chosen the subject to attack Hinduism, which was not true at all. Manik *da* had to clarify that the film was against the orthodoxy of religion and not against Hinduism per se.[14]

Though many critical studies have focused on the ideological conflict between the very dictatorial and fundamentalist Hindi Brahmin father Kalikinkar and his younger son Umaprasad, educated in more liberal Western studies, the real sacrificial goat is the deified young girl who Kalikinkar is determined to keep worshipping in a public space. Her husband does not have the mental strength or the courage to rescue her and bring her back to her private space even knowing that this might destroy his married life for good. The elder son Tarapada has no will of his own. He spends his days 'worshipping' his father and his nights on wine and women. So, when his father asks him to touch the feet of his own young sister-in-law, he does this. But the young woman, shocked at this sudden 'devotion', curls her toes, scratches her nails against the wall, and turns her face to the wall in shock, disgust and hate—for herself, for the state she is in, or for the ones touching her feet? His wife has no respect for him and generally does not allow him to come close to her.

Khoka, once closely attached to his aunt, is now scared of stepping into her shadow. In one scene, while he is at play, his ball rolls into the room in which Daya is resting. Daya waves at him to come in. He quickly runs in, picks up the ball and runs out without speaking to her. The soft smile on her face disappears. The ball is an object, a plaything for a child that once was a bridge between a child and an adolescent woman. Today, it is still a toy but the playmate is no longer recognised as one. *Devi* has touches of a Greek tragedy in which Kali, the destroyer, exacts her necessary sacrifice—through Khoka, through the death of Daya, and through the destruction of the Roy family, perhaps as 'punishment' meted out to an ardent devotee audacious enough to force a real woman to become a goddess. After Umaprasad sails away in a boat, the camera pans across the empty *thakurdalan,* the empty spaces that were filled with devotees hankering for their small dose of *charanamrita* and not one human soul is visible.

The lone sane 'voice' (more in silence than in articulation) is that of Harasundari, Daya's sister-in-law, who, right from the beginning, does not believe in this forced metamorphosis of the teenaged Daya from woman to goddess Kali. So, when her little boy Khoka falls ill, without her father-in-law's permission, she summons the country doctor. But the doctor hesitates to attend to the little patient without the patriarch's knowledge and permission. Harasundari is coerced to have Daya touch her sick child as she has already revived the life of a dying child. But Khoka dies in Daya's lap and Daya's life is destroyed forever.

When Umaprasad tries to take Daya to the city to rescue her from this enforced imprisonment, she is torn between her own growing conviction in her 'goddess-like' powers on the one hand and her vulnerable human-ness on the other. 'What if I am really a Devi? What if this brings you misfortune?' she asks, more of herself than of Umaprasad.

'Tumi jodi Debi hote tumi nije bujhte paarte na? Tumi ki tomar moddhe kono poriborton bujhte paro? Tomar ki mone hoy tumi manush now? Tumi amar stree now?' (But if you really were a goddess, wouldn't you be aware of it? Do you feel any changes within yourself? Don't you believe you are human anymore? Don't you think you are my wife?) Umaprasad implores, appealing to her rationality.

In the final sequence, when the unlikely goddess fails to save her beloved ailing Khoka—who is denied medical help by Kalikinkar, and is in turn, left at the mercy of Daya's divine prowess—she is reviled as a '*rakkhoshi*' (demoness) by her sister-in-law, who accuses her of devouring her son. In the penultimate scene, before Dayamoyee disappears into a misty field of smoke, she appears in a bedraggled trance, asking her husband to help her get dressed. The scene is cast in a pall of white, lending it a surreal, almost unearthly tenor.[15]

As Umaprasad tries to run away with her, they talk in whispers on the banks of the river in the village, while the tall blades of grass sway in the moonlight, reflecting their disturbed mental state and their still bodies. Dayamoyee, her *kajal* smeared around her eyes, her hair spread out around her, tears streaking down her scared face, her *bindi* blurred across her forehead, her body adorned in a lot of jewellery, spots the skeletal idol of the goddess Durga, half-immersed in water. This makes her question her credibility again as the goddess-incarnate. She goes back, turning away from the vast night landscape, silhouetted in the dark, filled with a mysterious air of foreboding. The escape boat can be seen in a long shot, shimmering in the distance. But the presence of the boat is futile. For Daya, there is just one escape—death.

In a flashback to their wedding night, Umaprasad jokingly characterises the shy, inarticulate Dayamoyee as an earthen doll *(mateer putul)* who cannot speak. Then, astounded by her beauty as he raises her veil, he calls her a *pratima,* a term used to describe both a beauteous object and the clay image of a goddess. Here Umaprasad is not speaking of divinity but of material beauty, which is why it is interesting that later in the story, when Dayamoyee sees the scattered clay of the idol on the river shore and refuses to be reduced to her material form, she registers her discomfort with this earlier erotic objectification.[16] But the allegorical links are clear: she is a beautiful, fourteen-year-old bride and then changed to become a clay idol as a human goddess installed in the *thakur dalan* of the ancestral home to be actually venerated as a living goddess who can bring a dying child back to life.

Ray is explicit in his critique of ideology as expressed through patriarchal family structures and Hindu religious orthodoxy in the film, but his critique is focused on the woman's sense of self and her degeneration into delusion and madness.[17]

Devi throws up a different facet of womanhood in a Bengal we are not familiar with except through literature. We accuse society and corporate interests such as the advertising world for objectifying the woman as a commodity in order to push sales of goods to which they may or may not be linked. But in *Devi*, we discover the eldest patriarch of a family satisfying his own 'devotional' interests by 'reducing' his daughter-in-law into an animated, live version of his favourite goddess Kali and vesting her with 'magic powers' she does not possess. For the first time in Indian cinema, Ray presented elaborately and in great detail, how the goddess can be exploited as a fetish when personified in the form of a beautiful woman who not only has no say in this shift, but does not even understand it.

MAHANAGAR METAMORPHOSIS OF THE HOUSEWIFE

Mahanagar is set in 1955. Ray's own move away from his joint family in 1948 was a forerunner of major shifts in Bengali society immediately following independence. *Mahanagar* was based on a short story by Narendranath Mitra titled *Abataranika*. Narendranath Mitra, who was alive then, is said to have thoroughly approved of Ray's script for the film. Large numbers of middle-class women are now working, and the joint family, as depicted in *Mahanagar*, has become the exception rather than the rule.[18]

The original story placed the husband at the centre. Ray shifted the emphasis to place it on the wife, Arati. This change of focus re-wrote the history of women in Indian cinema. It depicted the working wife in a lower middle-class family of Calcutta, her gradual autonomy in the face of economic pressures, and her changing status within the family by virtue of the change in her *status quo* via employment. By going beyond the realms of the original, Ray changed the entire perspective of the story. *Mahanagar* is Ray's personal statement on the changing values of the traditional, middle-class Bengali family of Calcutta. It is a microcosm of changes in urban, social and economic values. *Mahanagar* is a strong, positive and realistic statement on the socio-economic changes in urban Bengali life, more through the metamorphosis of Arati than through other characters in the film. Arati stands as both the sign and the signified of this slow but steady socio-economic evolution.

Mahanagar defines a marked departure in Ray's oeuvre till then. Before *Mahanagar*, his films were confined either to literary classics (*The Apu Trilogy*, *Devi*, *Parash Pathar*, *Jalsaghar*, *Teen Kanya*) or to a film based on his own script (*Kanchenjunga*). Though *Kanchenjunga* dealt with the urban Bengali of Calcutta, the Roy Choudhurys came of affluent and aristocratic stock. With *Mahanagar*, Ray took his first step inside a low middle-class Bengali family home.

Abataranika, the original story on which Mahanagar was based, was first published in the Puja festival issue of *Ananda Bazaar Patrika* in 1956.[19] The same year, the story found its place in a collection of short stories called *Chadai-Utrai* published by Mitra and Ghosh. Ray had read the story when he was making *Aparajito*. But Ray also derived source material from another short story by the same author entitled *Aakinchan* to flesh out the character of Arati's father-in-law Priyagopal, the retired schoolmaster in *Mahanagar*.

In an article in *Ekhhon* (1981) recalling his source for the film, Ray writes:[20]

> I wished to tinge the character of Arati's father-in-law with a more sentimental touch. In order to do this, I drew from another character from another Mitra short story. In this sense, *Mahanagar* is a blend of two short stories by the same author.

Creative changes

In the original story, Arati's father-in-law worked in the outer office of a *zamindar*. His character therefore, is cruder than Ray's portraiture drawn from another story. The original father-in-law's interaction with Arati was not exactly decent. So Ray cut this character out and replaced him with another old man from *Aakinchan*.

Ray also cut out the flashback in the original and set out the script in a straight chronological narrative. He invested the script with the cohesiveness the literary original lacked because of its telescopic narrative that moved backwards and forwards in time.

The third departure Ray made was in the characterisation of Arati's husband Subrata Majumdar, who is narrow-minded and suspicious in Mitra's story. Ray made him relatively broad-minded though he still suffers from problems of the male ego, finding it difficult to cope with a working wife when he is himself unemployed. The Subrata of Mitra's story could not digest his wife giving up a job to protest the humiliation and insult of her Anglo-Indian friend when she is sacked by her

Bengali boss. He tells his mother, 'The funny part of all this is that the one who has truly been insulted must have gone to the office puffing on her cigarette and already begun work. She is no sentimental fool!' Arati is shocked. She asks him, 'You too? You too are saying the same thing?' The story ends on a note that lucidly elaborates Subrata's insensitivity to his wife's empathy for her office colleague.

Ray's film ends on a positive and optimistic note, writing a complementary finish to Subrata's understanding and appreciation of his wife and the stand she has taken. Ray paints Subrata as a progressive man while he enlarges Arati's character to build her up as a great human being.

In the original story, Arati is left to cope with her decision alone, her husband having left her side and failed to support her. Her rebellion for a colleague from a different ethnic group brings her nothing more than loneliness. But Ray brings the story to a happy closure when the husband and wife walk out together to face the struggles of life, suggesting the togetherness that is a part of the urban Bengali middle-class' struggle to eke out a living in the city of Calcutta. When the film ends, both Subrata and Arati have joined the hundreds of jobless young people in the city. But they have emerged victorious in the battle of life together, and without fear.

Ray, explains Manabendra Saha,[21] was not just telling the story of a middle-class family of Calcutta. He used the Majumdar family in general and Arati, in particular, as a microcosm of a middle-class family trapped in the spidery web of conflicts, doubles complications through the shifts in the life and relationship between Arati and Subrata.

The most significant departure from the literary original is the shift of focus from Subrata in the original story to Arati in the film *Mahanagar*. It changes the entire perspective of the story that consequently lends itself to a feminist as well as a Marxist reading.

The film opens with a vignette of a lower middle-class family in the Calcutta of the mid-1950s. We meet the joint-family: Subrata Mazumdar (Anil Chatterjee), his wife Arati (Madhabi Mukherjee), their young son Pintoo, Subrata's unmarried sister Bani (Jaya Bhaduri), his father, a retired schoolmaster, and his mother.

Subrata Mazumdar, a bank employee, finds it difficult to provide for his large joint family with his meagre income. His father needs a new pair of prescription glasses, younger sister Bani's school fee is due, and mother needs a new can of *zarda* (chewing tobacco). Arati is like an anchor holding the family together. Subrata talks about a couple where the woman too is going to work. Soon, Arati makes up her mind to take up a job to supplement the household income. With some help from Subrata, and much against established custom and opposition of the elders, she finds a job of selling knitting machines door-to-door.

Going out to work, Arati discovers a new life. She proves successful in her work and gains self-confidence. Subrata now feels insecure and resentful. His father too puts pressure on his son to force Arati to quit the job. Subrata asks Arati to quit as he plans to earn more by moonlighting. The next morning, before Arati can give in her resignation, Subrata telephones her and asks her not to resign as he has lost his job.

Subrata suffers from all kinds of conflicting emotions as he watches his wife go out while he sits in bed and scans the jobs columns in newspapers. They begin to grow apart. Arati has found a new friend in a colleague Edith, an Anglo-Indian woman. Her boss does not like Edith because he considers her an offspring of 'our ex-rulers'. Blinded by prejudice, he accuses Edith of having been on leave of absence on false grounds, or loose morals and fires her. Arati asks her boss to apologise to Edith. He refuses and warns her about her own job. Arati hands over her old resignation letter and walks away.

Now neither Arati nor her husband has a job. On her way out, she meets Subrata. After the initial shock, they reconcile and are close to each other once again. Subrata understands her. Arati is hopeful that in such a big city, at least one of them is sure to find a job. As they walk into the city crowd, the camera tilts up to a street lamp lit up to herald the oncoming of evening while another holder beside the street lamp remains empty of a bulb.

Mahanagar is about the people of Calcutta. It enters into the privacy and the mindset of a family that sets off a chain of complicated relations resulting from the domesticated housewife transcending the private space of the household to step into the public space of the city's streets, the office and the houses of probable clients she visits as a saleswoman marketing knitting machines. Windows and mirrors show up reflections of the characters to themselves, to each other, to the city and to its people. The city comes across in brief glimpses—a small restaurant Arati steps into with a friend's husband; Subrata, her unemployed husband, sitting in the same restaurant hiding behind his newspaper and trying to catch snatches of his wife's interaction with this man; the lift taking her up to her office; Arati rushing down the flight of stairs in the end after she quits; the opening scenes when Subrata gets off the tramcar to come home as neighbourhood boys share an outdoor game; the chaos when Subrata is beaten up by the gathered crowd outside his bank; Arati's father-in-law's walking stick tumbling down the tall staircase of an eye specialist's chamber he had gone to for his new glasses; the salesgirls sitting together to exchange their experiences and tips on the job.

The city appears in framed images through windows opening up limitless possibilities that zero back into the confined spaces of the cluttered interiors of the Majumdar home. From the window in Arati's boss Mukherjee's spacious cabin, one gets a view of a growing Calcutta with multi-storey buildings coming up. The homes of the affluent families where Arati goes to market her knitting machines offer a glimpse into an elite Calcutta distanced from Arati's home in a narrow Calcutta bylane or Edith's small cubbyhole in an Anglo-Indian neighbourhood.

The sound design complements the city scenario, especially in the interiors suggesting dilemmas, choices and the possibilities open to the members of the family.[22] Do the Majumdar family members really have any choice? The narrative slowly unfolds the answer to this question. The use of light and shadow, brightness and darkness are symbolic. Reversals in everyday situations establish the changed situation of people in relation to each other.

The credits come up against shots of a cable-line atop a Calcutta tramcar with flashes of light emitting from the overhead wiring. The camera then zeroes into the tram to focus on Subrata Majumdar. He is wearing a coat over his shirt. Four points are established at once. One, the story is set in Calcutta; two, the time is morning; three, it is winter; four, it is centered on a man who commutes to work by tram, so he is a man of ordinary means.

In the closing shots, the camera explores the city in a long, tracking shot, starting with a wide-angle view of the whole scene and ending with a close-up of a street light, reminding us of the last shot in Antonioni's *The Eclipse*.

Arjun Appadurai writes about ethnoscapes (spaces produced through inflow of people such as immigrants, refugees), technoscapes (inflow of technology), finanscapes (flow of global capital, commodities), mediascapes (the repertoires of images and information) and ideoscapes (ideological shifts connected to Western world views).[23] These are different ways of looking at the global cultural flows strongly influenced by perspective, overlapping, and the rapidly shifting instability and mutability of global cultural flows. Madhuja Mukherjee adds that it is also important to study the cityscape or the structural changes that occur when immigration happens, or the physical shifts that take place (with globalisation of the economy and the culture) when flyovers, multi-storey buildings, or shopping malls are built by doing away with the existing habitat of the original residents—old houses, parks, water bodies, etc.[24] Or, when neon signs, digital billboards are erected like patchwork in the blue sky. Suddenly, the familiar spaces, the narrow lanes and by-lanes, the grocer's shop across the road, the old house built by ancestors are practically devoured by other geometric structures that invest the city with a kind of socio-political rebirth born out of the 'scapes' described by Appadurai. The nostalgia is tempered with a sense of history.

None of these 'spaces', it may be pointed out, apply to *Mahanagar*. Rather, it creates a different space altogether which perhaps may be termed socioscapes—spaces produced within the family as a result of a change in the work equation between and among men and women in a family.

The face of Calcutta that Mrinal Sen shows in *Padatik* reflects the violent spirit of the 1970s, now somewhat subdued 'like the lull after the storm,' writes Swapan Ghosh.[25] The hero of the story, effectively essayed by Dhritiman Chatterjee, is an

extremist who is hiding out in a well-appointed apartment of an elite lady who belongs to the glamourous world of advertising. The introspection during this space that he now has makes him realise that no leadership, no matter how radical and bold, can stand the test of time and efficacy unless questioned. He rebels against authoritarianism, true, but he does not really run away from the system. Sen keeps away from detailing the physical realities of the city. Yet, its presence is tangible in every frame of the film. The spirit of the city shapes the destiny of the characters and structures their feelings and beliefs. He comes out of his hideout when his ailing mother dies, and finds renewed hope when his father asks him to go on with the principles of change he believes in.

Mrinal Sen's *Kharij,* is another example. The film explores how the accidental death of a servant boy in the kitchen of a Kolkata-based family creates a sense of guilt in the minds of the husband and wife who employed him besides each trying to place the blame on the other. They are less concerned about the untimely and tragic death of a young boy than they are about the consequences the death might bring upon them. When the couple discovers that there will be no 'case' on this death resulting from their negligence, life goes on as if nothing happened. But does it, really? Sen keeps the question hanging in the air, begging an answer. Buddhadeb Dasgupta's *Dooratwa* is another example as is Aparna Sen's *36, Chowringhee Lane.*

Multiple readings of the text

Mahanagar can be seen from several perspectives:

(a) **A Marxist reading**: The film sheds light on the dual reproductive responsibilities of the woman who gives birth to the next generation (the little son who, in future will become an economically productive human being) and labours (through housework) for the current generation. Though her housework is comparatively marginalised, she still has some duties to perform. Her third dimension is that she is the only financial contributor to the household expenses soon after she takes up the job.

The patriarchal system has its material base in male control over woman's productive and reproductive labour through the institution called the family. Patriarchy and capitalism operate effectively together to use women as a profitable source of production and reproduction while keeping control over the woman's labour and perpetuating their inferior status. Subrata tries to exercise control over Arati by telling her to quit the job which he will try and compensate through moonlighting—some part-time job about which he has already spoken to a friend.

In terms of historical analysis of women's work, Marx and Engels[26] believed that earlier the men had a monopoly over the heavier work and that women were excluded from productive work outside the domestic sphere. This analysis ignores the work of women in mines, factories and on the land, as well as the work of peasant women and craftspersons. There is ample evidence to show that women have always engaged in social production. They perform not only wage work but reproductive work, or the whole gamut of work that is crucial for reproduction: cooking, cleaning, fuel preparation, gathering, gleaning for foods, etc. Women thus are not dependent on the income of their husbands, but the last guarantors of the survival of the family.[27]

R Delmar explored a different dimension of gender politics. To quote Delmar:

> If the origin of family constituted an achievement it was this, that it asserted women's oppression as a problem of history, rather than of biology, a problem which is the concern of historical materialism to analyse and revolutionary politics to solve.'[28] Hence, power tilted against women and weighted on men, that is the root cause of women's oppression and leads ultimately to conflict based on gender. Gender functions socially to meet structural and functional requirements. Ideology of gender, along the lines of this argument, is produced historically in cultural practices. Inequality between the sexes reinforces class inequality, while class divisions are accentuated by gender discrimination. Accordingly, class and gender are central to the analysis of women's oppression.[29] When separated from each other, class and gender can be crippling, but together they can be a powerful force. Separate, they have inherent limitations, but together, they provide a credible and viable framework to understand women's oppression.[30]

(b) **A Feminist Reading:** Socialist feminism analyses the power of men over women in terms of its class origin and patriarchal roots. 'In such an analysis, capitalism and patriarchy are neither autonomous systems, nor identical: they are mutually dependent.' Such a relationship between sex and class pitched in power or the converse, oppression, is termed capitalist patriarchy by Zillah Eisenstein.[31]

Arati's schism with Subrata smoothens out only when the two are at par—she too is jobless. Should one read between the lines to raise the question—would the chasm in the marriage have widened had Arati stayed with the job and had Subrata remained jobless?

In societies that are predominantly patriarchal and patrilineal, where women are discriminated against on grounds of sex alone, even women engaged in economically productive work derive power from the men in their lives and not from their own productive work. The husbands exercise the main veto in important decisions. In fact, women engaged in economically productive work often have less power than women *not* engaged in productive work. This happens in families where men are engaged in marginal occupations and do not have a strong economic base. They are insecure about their 'dominance' within the family and feel genuinely threatened by the substantial income of their wives.

In *Mahanagar*, Subrata takes the primary decisions—that Arati will take up a job; that she will have to quit the same job though her job brings economic security to the family because it becomes a cause of acute discomfort for him; that her wearing lipstick is not right; then, when his bank fails suddenly the day Arati is to hand in her resignation, he decides that she should not hand it in right now. He even writes out both the decisive letters—the letter of application and the letter of resignation—and asks Arati only to sign at the bottom. Arati knows how to read and write English. But the conditioning to be subjected to the husband's commands and directives without question is so deep-rooted that it does not even occur to her to do these simple things herself. Yet, at the end of it all, though her husband expressly tells her not to hand in her resignation, she decides otherwise not in defiance of her husband's command, but for another more individual and personal reason. Yet she walks out into the Calcutta evening hand-in-hand with husband Subrata, both without jobs, but content that the breach between them has healed.

Though the job brings out qualities within Arati that remained untapped when she was house-bound, it does not offer her the freedom of choice one would expect. It is the husband who accepts the fact that the wife must take up a job to supplement the meagre finances of the family. Till the point when her husband tries to stop her from resigning because he has suddenly become jobless, Arati is just a puppet in the hands of a seemingly democratic and 'understanding' husband who is actually as tradition-bound as the father from whom he is ideologically distanced. But with time, and with the vested responsibility of being the sole breadwinner, Arati unwittingly comes into her own, and ceases to be a puppet with the choice she makes following Edith's unfair dismissal.

There are other studies that treat the power of men and the subordination of women as effects of imperatives outside the direct relationship between the two. These arguments mainly explore the thesis of the reproduction of social structures as well as of bodies from generation to generation. Dorothy Dinnerstein in *The Mermaid and the Minotaur,* for example, argues that the power of men and the acquiescence of women stems from women's monopoly over early child rearing, which has been a historical necessity for mankind. Socialist feminists believe that the exploitation of women is connected to capitalism's drive for profit and its general need to reproduce itself—pressures that finally lead to a sex-divided work force and the oppression of the housewife. This point is absent in the power relations *Mahanagar* shows. But there is emotional exploitation in the way Arati is forcibly distanced by her husband who does not treat her kindly. Instead of acknowledging her contribution to the family in a time of financial crisis, he raises issues that are basically non-issues because he finds that the working world has made her happy instead of it being the other way round.

(c) **A Sociological Reading**: This emerges from the Calcutta backdrop against which the narrative is set. The tram car, the graffiti on the walls, the angry depositors at the bank, the interiors of the Majumdar's home, Edith Simmons' home with its typically cluttered Anglo-Indian décor, Arati's self-complacent and arrogant boss, the father-in-law's snobbish ex-student and his modern, fashionable, patronising wife, the affluent homes Arati visits to market her knitting machine defining the class distinctions within the Calcutta population, the barking Alsatian outside one of these homes, the cheerful camaraderie among the saleswomen—all point out to a richly textured collage of images in the backdrop, subtly reinforcing the message of a sociological transformation of the city, of its people in general and its women, in particular, emphasised by two images of two apparently polarised women—Arati Majumdar and Edith Simmons—representing two images of two different kinds of women rooted to the same city.

Within the marriage, Subrata changes too, as he discovers the happy expression on his wife's face when she comes home from work while he is forced to stay back at home. He sits smoking on his bed, reeling under the frustration of having to watch his wife take on the breadwinning role with contentment writ large on her face. Where does the money for his cigarettes come from? The answer is implicit in the change in the economic status of husband and wife within the family. From being a happily married man openly in love with his pretty wife, Subrata turns into an unhappy man who stoops to eavesdropping into a conversation between his wife and the husband of a friend of hers in a roadside tea-shop. Instead of approaching her upfront, he hides behind the newspaper he is reading, peeping out to see them walk out, talking cheerfully.

This scene shows another 'quality' Arati has acquired through her newly acquired status. When her friend's husband asks her what her husband does for a living, she smiles coyly and glibly lies with a single word: 'Business.' She bluffs her way through the conversation pretending that she has taken on a job just to while away her time. Subrata is concerned when he discovers that her vocabulary has changed. 'She no longer discusses domestic feminine issues with him but traditionally masculine issues like "sales", "salaries" and "commissions". She mentions Mukherjee's name more than her son's.'[32]

The cold war that initially began between Subrata and his father Priyagopal over Arati's taking up a job now spills over into his relationship with Arati. Arati however, remains unaware of this change in her husband, till he questions her about the stick of lipstick hidden in her purse when she asks him to take some money out of it to pay someone. He tells her to give up her job at one point, saying that he will manage with moonlighting, and though Arati is quite reluctant to give up what she has just begun to enjoy, she signs the letter he drafts and puts it in her purse. Ironically, when she is ready to hand in the letter to her boss, the circumstances are dramatically different. The question arises about Subrata's pushing his wife to quit her job. What makes him do it? Is it because it makes the domestic sphere suffer from her absence with his mother and sister having to share the chores between them? Is it because *her* going out to work makes *him* feel less powerful? Or, is it because he suffers from a sense of discomfort when he finds that she is actually enjoying what she is doing and is not really doing it out of the force of circumstance that drove her to the job in the first place? The answer is left open for the audience.

Many scenes bring out ambiguity, contradiction and harmony at many moments in the narrative. Images transform one meaning into another through light, mirror reflections, windows offering a glimpse of the cityscape, visual reversals suggesting plurality and continuity. When Arati clambers down the stairs of the office and informs Subrata of her decision to quit her job, he praises her decision and accepts that he would perhaps not have had the guts to take a similar one. From a close-up of the couple, the camera tilts up towards the city outside to rest on the street lamp as the couple walk under it to mingle into the crowds below. Is it a light of hope? One cannot be sure because there is also an empty holder without any bulb in it.

The closing shot smoothens out the fracture in the marriage brought in by Arati's employed status vis-à-vis Subrata's unemployed one. The film closes on this note of courage—they are sure their Calcutta will soon find them jobs, and hope—as long as they are together, fear and uncertainty are superfluous emotions.

Conclusion

Mahanagar introduces the Indian audience, perhaps for the first time, to a woman who is awakened to the possibility of determining the course of her life. Chidananda Dasgupta strikes a note of dissent by pointing out how Arati loses her freedom when she quits her job. He says that her awakening comes from the husband:

> For men have been traditional liberators of women. But traditionally too, they have retracted when they have found the consequences of their action undermining their overlordship…When she hands in her resignation, it is not in obedience to her husband's wish, but to her own impulsive fellow-feeling for the Anglo-Indian girl

> who is unjustly dismissed. It is her one act of protest against society, and she carries it out in a sphere where she means something in her own right. Ironically enough, in this act, she also gives up the freedom she has won.[33]

Dasgupta goes on to point out that Ray's closure showing the husband and wife meeting under the doorway where the husband says, 'Do not worry. It is a vast city and one of us is bound to find a job' provides too pat a solution to a problem that will continue to plague us for a long time to come. *Mahanagar,* in other words, lacks the strong, open-ended closure of Ray's *Charulata.*

Ray proves through *Mahanagar*—genuinely a Ray creation than a Narendra Mitra one—what he himself thinks of characterisation in his films. He once said:

> Somehow I feel that a common person—an ordinary person who you meet everyday on the street—is a more challenging subject for cinematic exploration than persons in heroic moulds, either good or bad. It is the half-shades, the hardly inaudible notes that I want to capture and explore.

The timelessness and universality of *Mahanagar* can neither be denied, nor underestimated. The real tension within Arati remains a perennial one. The inner conflict is not about whether she should or should not take up a job, but whether she should try and please everyone—husband, child and in-laws, boss, clients—or whether she should only please herself. For the Indian woman, the conflict can be particularly acute, because those close to her expect more than is expected of women in the West, writes Andrew Robinson.[34] Arati's husband tells her, with an affectionate smile, 'A woman's place is in the home.' Expressed in English as it is in the film, the line offers an authentic sample of a Victorian value system that held true in more orthodox circles in Calcutta during the time-frame of the film.[35] For the first time, Ray deals with an ordinary woman, who, one fine day, finds herself thrown out into the world, trying to make both ends meet for the extended family she belongs to. The family is sandwiched between the social hypocrisies of the low middle class and an impending financial crisis.

Arati proves that a woman has vast resources of inner strength, which she herself is unaware of. She draws upon these resources when the time is right, when she discovers that patriarchy, which defines a society dominated by men, has failed to solve emerging socio-economic problems that have a bearing on the family to begin with, then on the economy, and finally, on the culture.

CHARULATA THE LITERARY LIAISON

There is a kind of monotony in the way women within the family are typecast into clichéd models of plastic human beings in cinema, and to some extent, in literature as well. Generally speaking, the two extremely polarised images of women we are familiar with are: (1) the chaste, docile and submissive woman who is conditioned to martyr herself for any cause linked to the family, and (2) the unchaste, vile and voluptuous woman whose values are diametrically opposed to the values held sacrosanct by the former. The former is placed on a pedestal and celebrated while the latter is condemned and ostracised. Sadly, the grey areas do not seem to exist for the average filmmaker. Both categories of women can easily be reduced to the lowest common denominator of being stripped of choice, and of exploring spaces within which they can grow beyond the parameters the family rigidly fixes them in. Much of the blame for the perpetuation of these clichéd celluloid images of womanhood and wifehood in cinema lies on the shoulders of male filmmakers—across the world in general and in India in particular.

Ray's *Charulata* (1964) is based on *Nastaneer* (The Broken Nest) an 80-page novelette written by Tagore in 1901. Its translator, Mary M Lago, describes it as 'one of Tagore's best works of fiction.'[36] The story of the film and the original literary piece takes place in 1879, at a time when the Bengal Renaissance was almost at its peak. Western thoughts of freedom and individuality were just about to ruffle the age-old calm feathers of a feudal society. Thinking men were responding to it and some changes were already in motion. Women's liberation was being talked about, but not beyond a few cases of widow-remarriage and education. In Charu of *Charulata*, Ray probably discovered the crystallisation of the Indian woman, poised between tradition and modernity. Intelligent, sensitive, graceful and serene, Charu was a traditional woman whose psyche imbibed waves from the world outside as her British-influenced husband Bhupati celebrated the victory of the Liberals in Britain. It was a time when nineteenth century Western social philosophy and Ram Mohan Roy's ideas were fired by the liberation of women.

The artist has the right to look anywhere for his material—and if he finds his stories and characters in books rather than in life, if he finds his *donee* on a printed page rather than in a glimpse of a painting or an overheard piece of conversation,

so be it. There is a natural impulse to want to vivify a work of literature that has moved us. The challenge of adaptation itself might excite the filmmaker and that may inspire him to discover new techniques, new strategies, expand the narrative and psychological possibilities of his art. The history of film suggests that adaptations have been quite as revolutionary in their techniques—if not more so—than other types of film. Chidananda Dasgupta insists that a film adapted from literature 'would contain something of the chemistry of the mind of the filmmaker.' He says that not only would some aspects of incidents and characters undergo a change, 'but the very composition of the elements, the molecular structure if you like, would undergo a transmutation.'[37]

Cinema, being an eclectic art form, has borrowed generously from earlier art forms like music, poetry, painting and architecture. The reverse has also been true. Novelists too, have learnt a lot from cinema. In a letter to Murari Bhaduri (brother of theatre legend Sisir Kumar Bhaduri) in 1929, Tagore stated that the flow of images constitutes cinema. This flow, he wrote, should be used so that it can communicate without the help of words. 'The cinema (*chhayachitra*, in his words) is still enslaved to literature,' he wrote, and attributed this 'dependence' to the general ignorance of the masses to which cinema caters.[38]

Cinema has the inherent ability to transcend the constraints of literature.[39] Ray's films reveal how, even through a veritable 'mutation' of his literary source, he has produced the purest conceivable cinema. 'It is astonishing how deeply he absorbs the works of Bibhutibhushan Bandopadhyay and Tagore (*The Apu Trilogy*, *Charulata*, etc.) digesting them in as much the same way as the young man in *Parash Pathar* (The Philosopher's Stone) finds the stone disappearing into his system with his high metabolism.'[40]

In his writings, Ray has stressed the visual essence of cinema. In one of the more familiar passages, he claims that he looks for visual transitions between shots rather than speech or sound connections. While defending his adaptations of classics, he comes back to this question to explain the liberties taken with literary texts. In *Charulata Prasange*, Ray gives a minutely detailed account of the processes a literary narrative must go through if one is to acknowledge the specificities of the cinematic medium:

> A montage of shots shows Charu writing the short story, then carrying a copy of the journal in which it has been published, to show it to Amal, who sits at a desk. She beats him over the head with it and shows him what she has achieved. She defiantly takes a small key from the desk at which he sits and throws it out of the window. While he reads, she goes out of the room and tells Manda, 'You put so much spice in Amal's that it burns his mouth. I'll make it myself.' She goes to her bedroom and sits on her bed, making *paan* in a state of defiant anger. She collects the pair of embroidered slippers (made originally for Bhupati) from the dresser, and takes them, together with the *paan*, back to Amal. She approaches him and puts the *paan* in his mouth.

> Seizing the copy of the journal, she angrily throws it across the room, out of his reach. 'What are you doing?' asks Amal. Charulata moves towards the window, trembling with emotion. 'Don't you realise how good your writing is?' Amal goes on. Charu rushes towards Amal, buries her head in his arms, weeping. 'I won't write anymore,' she cries. After a few moments, she moves away from him, a little awkward now and says, 'How silly I am. Now your shirt is all wet.' She nervously toys with a round object on the desk, gathers up the journal, then departs, leaving Amal to ponder over her behaviour.[41]

This scene does not exist in Tagore's original story, nor does the story contain any comparable scene. Why then, did Ray write it in? This five-minute sequence, writes Ray, is an example of the power of compression of the cinematic medium. It explains several things at the same time, which a work of literature will need pages to describe, and then too, may not be able to capture with the same intensity. According to Ray himself, these are:

(a) Charu's literary talents are greater than Amal's own;
(b) Charu's intention in getting published in a prestigious magazine is not to get published per se, but rather to prove to Amal that she is better qualified than Mandakini (to whom she suspects Amal is getting attracted);
(c) By snatching the *paan* box from Mandakini's hands, she tries to prove that she has the right over Amal and that

Mandakini has no 'right of entry' into the world of Amal and Charu;

(d) Charu's gifting Amal with the pair of slippers originally embroidered for husband Bhupati is the first hint of her indifference and neglect towards Bhupati. Ray adds that the original *Nastaneer* has many such examples of neglect written into it by Tagore.[42]

Though *Charulata*, the film, is distanced from *Nastaneer*, it does not move away completely from the original in terms of the essence of the Tagore story. Amitabh Chattopadhyay has disputed Ray's loyalty to the essence of Tagore's original story.[43] But when one considers the relocation of the story, crafted by Ray almost a hundred years after Tagore wrote it, one begins to understand the perspective of a filmmaker 'looking' at a story that was penned by a different person (Tagore) in 1901 (about five characters set in 1879) through his 'cinematic' vision which is—and has to be—distanced from Tagore's literary vision.

Yet, there is this sense of 'reverence' to the master-litterateur Ray expresses through other visual components in the film. The recreation of the period to create the *mise-en-scene* and the setting is an example. The European style *haveli* with its heavy, ornate furniture is made into a gilded cage for the helpless Charu. Long corridors, rooms seen through vistas, shuttered windows, dark wallpaper, all combine to create an overpowering presence of being enclosed in a confined space, while at the same time offering glimpses of dappled sunlight filtered through the central courtyard or in the formal garden.

They also highlight the loneliness and the boredom that defines Charu's life. To quote from Chidananda Dasgupta:

> The exquisite period flavour is Ray's own, and distinguishes the film from the story which Tagore takes for granted. The sunlit garden, the swing, the embroidery, the floral motifs on the doors and walls, the horse-drawn carriage, the evocative settings created by Bansi Chandragupta are, however, more than exquisite decorations; they frame the action and set it at a distance—the distance of contemplation.[44]

But it is this very 'distance of contemplation' marking the 'process of transportation' which makes *Charulata* a creative cinematic expression that stands independent of its original source, much as it takes the original Tagore story a bit further ahead in time. The 'process of transportation' from the novelette to the film both necessitates as well as creates the

'changes' that purist critics of *Charulata* question.

The 'swing' sequence for instance, does not exist in Tagore's story. It forms an important setting for the growing relationship between Charu and Amal, the subtle changes within the relationship, and the different functions 'writing' plays in it. Besides offering Charu her own point of view. The swing became a very important and vital element in the film.[45] Tagore's original story finds Bhupati departing in the end, leaving the wife to her grief. Ray opts for a more realistic solution of bringing them together again to live forever in a state of suspended animation.[46] Bhupati, after realising Charu's true feelings for Amal upon their return from Puri, rushes out of the room before Charu sees him. He goes for an aimless ride in his carriage and as he tries to stifle his tears with the handkerchief embroidered by Charu, he notices the first initial of his name, 'B' delicately embroidered by Charu. The handkerchief is still there. But the relationship between the giver and receiver has changed. He tucks it back into his pocket. He comes back. Charu, now in control of her emotions, puts forth a hand in welcome. He extends his hand, but they do not meet, since time freezes the moment in eternity.[47] Their inner separation is eternal though to outward appearances, they are still man and wife.[48]

Had Tagore written this same story in 1964, when Ray made the film, perhaps he too, would have closed his story along similar lines. The same logic would apply to Ray's strong visual statement intensifying and highlighting the loneliness of Charu understated in the original story. *Charulata*, the film, takes the argument of a young married woman's loneliness and subsequent attraction for her brother-in-law Amal further, to fit into the social realities of the 1960s, without changing the framework of the time and the place given in the Tagore story.

Literature as a leitmotif

The functions of reading, writing and rhyming with literature, converting literature into visual motifs to complement the cinematographic narrative, play a uniquely significant role in *Charulata*. Writing is a major thematic focus in both the film and the novelette.[49] *Charulata* is a unique example of Ray's relentless search for literary signs of all kinds to create a semiotic universe where the story can be embedded. Cinematic detailing in this sense takes on a completely new meaning.[50]

(i) **Reading:** Charu, Amal and Bhupati love reading. Amal and Bhupati are well-read in arts, literature, politics and music. Charu is mainly self-educated. Bhupati's universe is distanced from the reading universe of Charu and Amal. The suited, booted and bearded Bhupati is inspired by the gospels of Mills and Bentham, Macaulay, Garibaldi and Edmund Burke, by ideas of freedom and equality. Despite this influence of political philosophers of the European Renaissance, Bhupati is untouched by the revolutionary changes in literature, beginning with Shakespeare, to Shelley and Byron.

Amal appears to have been influenced more by the works of Emerson, though he is conversant with the poetry of Byron. In Bengali, his taste in reading finds common ground with Charu. Both Amal and Charu are fond of Bankim Chandra

Chattopadhyay. Soon after the film opens, covering footage of seven minutes sans dialogue, Charu, browsing through the bookshelf, sings his name over and over: 'Bankim, Bankim.' When Amal arrives, he enters singing *Hare Murare Madhukaitbharey*…a patriotic battle-cry picked from the Bankim Chandra classic *Ananda Math*. He rushes in along with the storm raging outside, and his 'battle-cry' here sounds like a cry of joy and victory, spurred on by his spirit of youth and freedom.

His first line in the film is a question to Charu. He asks, '*Bouthaan,*[51] have you read Bankim Chandra's *Ananda Math*?' 'Yes,' she answers. In the same scene, Bankim's essay, *Prachina O Nabina* is used in a question-answer form between Amal and Mandakini, who, as ignorant as she is, when asked which slot she falls into, answers '*Jaani naa*' (I don't know). *Prachina* means 'ancient woman' and '*Nabina*' means 'modern woman'. This dialogue is introduced by Ray here to establish (a) the difference in the intellectual and emotional psyche of the two women, Mandakini and Charulata (b) Amal's obvious fondness for Bankim Chandra (c) Amal's 'slotting' of the two women. This is 'a paradigmatic statement on the women's question in the nineteenth century' introduced in the dialogue.'[52]

Soon after the film opens, a scene goes like this:

> Charu and her husband are conversing at night. 'Charu feels very lonely, isn't it?' Bhupati asks Charu. 'I've got used to it,' Charu replies. 'The habit of getting used to loneliness is not a good habit,' says Bhupati. Then, as Charu begins to search for a book in the bookshelf, she

> asks him, 'Have you read *Svarnalata*?'[53] Bhupati laughs. Charu raises her eyes to meet his, and asks, 'Why are you laughing?' Bhupati comes close to Charu, looks down at her beautiful face and says, 'I have Charulata, I do not need dramas or novels.' He draws Charu close to him. Charu rests her head on his shoulder and they move towards the bedroom.

The dialogue subtly points out the difference between Bhupati's and Charu's way of looking at the novel. While Charu wishes to learn more about his taste for fiction (trying to find with her husband, some common ground for interaction), Bhupati equates a 'creative work of literature' with 'a thing of beauty.' In so doing, he reduces both *Svarnalata* and *Charulata* to objects of no importance apart from the fact that their names rhyme. Charu is not a 'book' just as *Svarnalata* is not a flesh-and-blood woman. Nor is Charu just 'a thing of beauty' as Bhupati's way of holding her close and looking at her suggests. This apparent 'closeness' is undercut by the inner 'distance' between husband and wife. Despite his apparent intellectualism, progressive thinking and fondness for British 'liberal' ways, Bhupati still thinks that a woman's main essence lies in her beauty. And that he does not care for the kind of fiction Charu reads.

(b) Writing: Bhupati writes politics only in English. Amal and Charu write in Bengali. The topics they write on, however, are not the same. Charu, when she writes, chooses 'My Village.'[54]

Charu writes strictly for private exchange, through which she can 'write herself' into the literary discourse.[55] Amal writes on topics like 'The Light on a Moonless Night,' or 'The Darkness of the Afternoon,' about abstractions, frothy and verbose, conditioned by things he learnt at school and college. In this sense, his writing is distanced from the lay reader. Charu's writing is closer, not only to the lay reader, but also to the earth. Her style is simple but mature. In effect, Charu's article is published in *Biswabandhu*, a far more prestigious magazine than *Sarorooha*, the magazine which publishes Amal's piece. The purpose of their writing is also at variance. While Amal writes with the confidence that he has the talent, Charu writes as if in vengeance for the 'betrayal of trust' Amal demonstrates by sending off his article for publication against her explicit instructions not to do so. Amal writes for public acceptance in a public vehicle of some prominence.

Charu begins to write to prove to Amal that (a) she is qualitatively a better woman than Mandakini, whom she feels jealous of and (b) what Amal can do, she can do better. So, she suddenly decides to write an article and sends it to *Biswabandhu*. Their respective reactions to their articles when they are published, are in sharp contrast. Amal is thrilled about his article's acceptance. But he gives this information to Mandakini and not to Charu. Though he apologises to Charu, he also expects her to respect his talent as a good writer. When Charu's piece is published, her reactions are described in detail earlier on in this paper. She announces that she will never ever write again. Because her purpose has been served.

She need not write any more. There are two letters in the film, penned by Amal for Bhupati, once when he leaves the house, then again when Bhupati and Charu return from Puri and find the envelope waiting for them at the table. These too, play a dramatic role in the unfolding of the conflicts within the three persons in the film. The letter, the act of writing, the written page—these weave a pattern of their own.[56]

For Charu, writing covers a wide horizon of spaces, as follows:

(a) She explores the cerebral spaces of her intellect and her creativity through the very act of writing;

(b) She explores the emotional spaces of time and memory through her choice of subject: 'My Village';

(c) She transcends the geographical and social spaces a housewife like her is confined to by sending off her article to a prestigious publication like *Biswabandhu*;

(d) She appropriates her own space in a completely different time, place and social setting without leaving her original

world—with her article and her byline printed in the pages of *Biswabandhu*;

(e) She demonstrates complete control over this self-created space by declaring that she will never write again.

(c) The Sound Leitmotif: Literature makes its strong presence felt when Charu and Amal indulge in an alliterative game. This begins in a scene shot in Charu's bedroom. Their dialogue is an interesting banter focusing on the letter *ba* (B in English) from the Bengali alphabet. All the words used in this amusing banter that begins to change in mood and direction along the way, have Bengali words beginning with 'b'. These are: Bilet (England), Bristol, Bengalis, Burdwan, *biye* (marriage), barrister, back to Bengal, *baapbaap* (Gosh!), *byas* (Is that enough?) Bankim, Bishvriksha, *Bouthaan* and *beesh* (poison.) This entire banter is backed by vividly eloquent visuals of Amal and Charu, changes in the tone, pitch and clarity of their voices as they engage in this seemingly innocent banter which changes mood as they go along. This is one of several scenes which clearly shows Charu's irresistible attraction for Amal and Amal's confused, uncertain and timid reactions to her somewhat direct overtures.

(d) Word as Visual: As the film opens, we see an image of Charu's hands in close-up, embroidering the alphabet 'B' (for Bhupati) over the length of the title shot, signalling the significance of the written word in the film. It is a world that is already textually worked upon, embroidered, that Ray has chosen to be his material. The 'B' here is ornamentally decorated with flowers, in keeping with the graphic style Ray used for designing his logo for the title of the film, *Charulata*, and the original name *Nastaneer*. 'B' here is more a visual than a letter. The same handkerchief with 'B' appears thrice over the film, each time with a different significance in the lives of both Charu and Bhupati.

When the film opens, Charu is the loyal, devoted wife, embroidering her husband's handkerchief lovingly with his monogram. The same night, she coyly holds the handkerchief, the embroidery complete, against her chest, and waits outside the room where Bhupati is busy writing his editorial. It is as if she is inviting him to their bedchamber, so that the night is not wasted away in forced solitude. He understands the message but asks her to wait for a couple of minutes. 'I didn't come for that,' says Charu and holds the handkerchief out to him. The last time, Bhupati takes out the same handkerchief to wipe away his tears of grief, shock and betrayal when he discovers Charu's feelings for Amal. But he stops when he discovers the letter 'B' on it. The three uses of the same handkerchief in three different time-and-place contexts spell out the metamorphosis in the relationship between Bhupati and Charu. This effectively reverses the conventional word-versus-vision scenario that sustains between literature and cinema. Ray establishes a metaphoric dialectic between the two, word and visual, by using the letter 'B' as a visual. The ornately decorated register Charu prepares for Amal and then writes his full name '*Sree Amal Kumar Bosu*' in her own beautiful hand, is another example of turning word into visual.

Ray's designing of the masthead for Bhupati's paper, *The Sentinel*, illustrates his visual fondness for the beauty of graphics. 'It is a very old typeface. I don't remember now. We had printed a number of copies of the paper…I had even asked people to preserve a copy. It was my typeface. But I modelled it on some old newspapers stored in the National Library archives,' explained Ray in an interview.

(e) **Smelling Literature:** Bhupati is so enchanted by the power of the printed word that he enjoys the smell of the ink on fresh paper in his newly printed issue of *The Sentinel*. His paper, he says, is Charu's co-wife (because it takes him away from Charu.) Later, in that dramatic moment when Charu tries to hide the shock and pain of Amal having sent off his article to *Sarorooha* and picking on Mandakini to be the first one to hear of it, she locks herself in her room and refuses to open the door to Amal. When Bhupati comes knocking, she opens it with her back to him, to hide her tears. Bhupati does not bother to see her face, and asks her to smell his new paper. Charu smells it and Bhupati walks away, oblivious to the storm in his wife's life.

(f) **Reference from Literature:** The film almost wallows in the proliferation of references to authors of all kinds: Taraknath Gangopadhyay, Rammohan Roy, Shakespeare, Byron, Steele, Emerson. It also introduces the author Tagore himself into the story—through his songs—constantly hummed, sung, or played in the background. On the last freeze shot, the name of the original story is superimposed in one corner of the frame: *Nastaneer*. Does this suggest that the 'broken nest' will take on from this point? Because it appears where other films have the 'The End' sign. Is it a suggestion of the 'end' of *Charulata* and the 'beginning' of *Nastaneer*? Where the 'woman' ends and the breaking of her 'nest' begins? There is this clear picture of the process in which the literary sign actually produces the visual instead of the word being used to 'explain' the image, either before, or during, or after the image flashes on screen.

Conclusion

In *Charulata*, Ray uses a whole array of 'feminine' objects and turns them around to mean different things at different times. The handkerchief with the delicately embroidered 'B' and the pair of slippers Charu was embroidering for Bhupati (but later presented to Amal) are ironic comments on the hypocrisy within a feudal marriage by negotiation where the man and woman are totally unmatched. The lorgnette's use has been explained in detail already. The *paan* and the *paan* box reveal Charu's fiercely possessive feelings for Amal and offer her an excuse to 'touch' him by stuffing his mouth with *paan*. The swing too, generally associated with women during the time-place setting of the film, is heavy with meaning and yet, never appears loaded. It connotes a change in pace, rhythm and movement in Charu's life. Later, when she sits on the swing alone, she uses it as her 'thinking prop' so to say, as she draws from childhood memories to write her first and last article.[57]

Amal's register for writing, lovingly prepared and decorated by Charu, is her way of saying that his literary pursuits are exclusively for her eyes alone. The kaleidoscope, which fills the screen with its rhythmic beauty, which Mandakini enjoys looking at but Charu ignores, subtly hints at the difference between the two in their source of joy. When Amal too, enjoys looking through the kaleidoscope, it is a pointer to the fact that perhaps, Amal is intellectually and emotionally closer to Mandakini than to Charu.

A passage in Tagore's novelette *Nastaneer* reads: 'Perhaps Bhupati had the usual notion that the right to one's own wife's affection does not have to be acquired. The light of her love shines automatically, without fuel, and never goes out in the wind.'

Ray introduces the 'wind' in the form of a storm, three times in the film, each time linking it in some way to Charu and Amal. From afar, one can hear the shattering of glass somewhere, when Amal arrives, and again in the end, when Charu reads the letter and breaks down. And nothing is the same any more. Not for Charu alone, for all of us who identify with her pain knowing fully well that it is not our own.

MAINSTREAMING OF PROSTITUTES IN THREE RAY FILMS

Depiction of prostitution on celluloid has a hidden charisma of its own for the masses. It is a part of everyday sexism. But in constructing certain specific representations of women, it codes women as an object of the male gaze. It must be recalled here that the prostitute, on celluloid as in real life, has her saleability in certain manners of speaking and understanding, with other more readily available and culturally prevalent representations of women. Indian directors, both men and women, are yet to invent new codes of non-voyeuristic vision.

There are four chief areas in the discourse of prostitution in real life, in literature and in cinema. These are: (a) the prostitute as a subject, or the agency-issue as it is called; (b) the prostitute as the object, analogous to a slave, who has been coerced into the profession, and is therefore, a victim: whether of an organised prostitution trade, or of specific agents of force and oppression, or widespread economic circumstances; (c) the prostitute and her sexuality; and (d) the prostitute as a working woman like any other, in an essentially capitalist, but democratic state. As the above analyses reveal, for the most part, Indian cinema has focussed on the victim identity of the prostitute rather than on her agency. This is what finds the greatest audience sympathy, has greater commercial value, is the least complex and offers scope for both romance and titillation.

We take a look at how Satyajit Ray treated prostitution rather than the prostitute as just one more cog in the massive wheel called life. She is trapped in a market where she is the product being sold and bought, even within the corporate world where she can be used as a bribe to close a possibly profitable deal.

Though the distinctions between women who are prostitutes and women who are not are sharply and explicitly drawn in social negotiations and interactions, the slippages between the two categories are frequent and significant in theory, argument and practice. The contractual terms of bourgeois marriage; many women's confessions to 'occasional prostitution' or sex for favours; the forms of heterosexual 'dating'; the description of women accused of promiscuity as 'whores': these provide examples of the blurring of categories of respectable bourgeois womanhood and the prostitute, otherwise maintained in sharp distinction from each other.[58] The recognition of continuities among women is central to any understanding of prostitution even while we are attending to the specificities of the phenomenon in our endeavours to see and understand how prostitution is represented in Indian cinema, mainly of the popular variety.

Ray has taken the sex worker out of traditional ghettoes like Sonagachhi and Harkata Goli to place her within mainstream society where her vocation is rendered 'invisible' and therefore, becomes mainstream. In India, approximately ten million women are sex workers and live off their earnings from prostitution; they are not only ill-paid but their earnings swallowed up by an entire chain of 'agents'. This is not a legalised profession and is similar to the selling of contraband liquor and trafficking in women and girls that continue to flourish across the crevices and dark alleys of every Indian city, small town and village. Says social activist Jasodhara Mukherjee, 'Sonagachi once witnessed at least 15,000-20,000 clients every day, though it has come down very much during the pandemic since last year.'

Durbar, an organisation in Kolkata, looks after the education of the children of sex workers, organises medical camps, spreads awareness about AIDS and other STDs, helping with micro-finance and savings and so on, and has a large membership that purportedly is politically neutral. Durbar, which means unbeatable or unstoppable, represents 65,000 sex workers (male, female and transgender) and is active in identifying and challenging the underlying socio-structural factors that help perpetuate stigma material deprivation and social exclusion of sex workers. Its mission is 'to build a world where all marginalised communities live in an environment of respect, rights and dignity'.

But the sex workers portrayed by Ray in three of his films would never have been in the register of an organisation like Durbar because for the common man, they just do not 'exist'.

In *Ashani Sanket* (Distant Thunder, 1973) Chhutki, a poor girl from a lower caste, is pulled into the trade by her hunger which the scar-faced brickfield agent promises to fulfil at a time when basic food is absent. The film is set in 1943 Bengal when the British rulers began to hoard rice to feed its soldiers arriving

to fight World War II. When the only Brahmin's wife Ananga, who Chhutki is very fond of, guesses that she is sleeping with the scar-face for some rice, she is angry and refuses Chhutki's offer of rice from her 'earnings.'

'What can I do? I always feel hungry,' she says, turning away. She runs away to the city with the scar-face because her hunger decimates the moral values which have been inculcated in her. We know she will be trafficked into prostitution but we do not know whether that will fulfil her craving for food.

The common thread running through Ray's treatment of prostitution is its organic evolution as an integral, indivisible and unavoidable act within the evolution of a society now dotted with greed, lust, consumerism and corruption—not necessarily in that order.

Ashani Sanket is based on Bibhutibhusan Bandopadhyay's noted novel on the Bengal famine. Chhutki, unlike Moti who dies of starvation, or Ananga, who adjusts to the grim reality, is prepared to exchange favours for a fistful of rice from a hideous, scarred man she might never have looked at in normal circumstances. Conditioned morals of a patriarchal society mean little to Chhutki when hunger stares her in the face. She runs away to the city, ostensibly to disappear into one of its red-light areas. Women like Chhutki are not a minority in contemporary India. Ray, perhaps, can be credited with the first non-voyeuristic but aesthetic and sensitive vision of prostitution in India presented in fictional cinema. She voluntarily walks out of the mainstream to step into the strange world of sex work in the belief that at least she will not die of hunger.

Material deprivation has been portrayed as the main motive behind the entry of the heroine into the profession of a sex worker. Polly Adler, an infamous brothel madam, in her autobiography, *A House is Not a Home*, writes: 'When a fifteen-year-old girl looks around her with the new awareness of adolescence and sees only poverty and ugliness, the ground work is laid.' This is illustrated lucidly in *Ashani Sanket* and *Jana Aranya*.

In *Pratidwandi* (The Adversary, 1971) Ray introduces his audience to a different kind of sex worker. She holds a job as a qualified nurse who moonlights as a sex worker. Much against his will, the hero Siddhartha Choudhury, who drops out of medical college due to his father's sudden death, is introduced to this woman by his friend, Adinath. In every move, we find he is distinctly uncomfortable in her presence and surprised to find that she is actually a nurse. Is Siddhartha scared to reveal in his friend's presence that he is a virgin? Or is his discomfort rooted in the fact that he is not easy in the company of females?

The lady does not use the kind of language a hard-core sex worker is expected to use. She speaks in a flirtatious, even mocking tone, displays her long hair, comes out in a bra and petticoat and allows her covering to come off. When she finds that Siddhartha is nervous and shaky, she asks him for a cigarette, asking him to light it for her and tells Adinath that his friend does not like her at all. She is quite open about her double life and it appears that she manages to keep the two occupations apart.

The role was portrayed by Miss Shefali, who had earned sobriquets like 'Bengal's Helen' and the 'Queen of Cabaret' because of her entry into the cabaret scenario at a time when the white-skinned cabaret dancers were slowly fading away. She did act in a few films but she made her name as a cabaret dancer. She earned very handsomely but in the long run, due to her innate philanthropic nature, she lost it all to whoever came to her for help and died in penury, alone and old.

This woman, the nurse who moonlights as a sex worker whose name we do not know, is not into prostitution out of poverty but for some extra income. But we do not know that. Perhaps she has a family to take care of and the single source of earning is not enough. Ray offers us a glimpse into the rapidly changing scenario in Calcutta where an educated man like Siddhartha cannot land a job despite a good interview, where he suspects his own sister of selling herself to become a model, or compromising with her boss and where a qualified nurse takes sex work as just one more source of earning.

In *Pratidwandi*, the nurse does not belong to any local 'ghetto' that prostitution as a profession defines because to all outward appearances, and officially, she is a nurse. Her sex work is a 'side business' hidden from public view and clients arrive mainly through word-of-mouth. She does not seem to have an 'agent' or a pimp. In this sense, she flows with the mainstream and appears happy.

Ray's *Jana Aranya* (The Middleman, 1975) is a scathing comment on erosion of values arising partly out of a decadent education system and partly out of unemployment and associated corrupt practices encroaching into the lives of the urban middle-class.

As the hero Somnath, along with his friend, goes door to door to search for a woman for the 'reward' of a prized contract, Ray, with his subtle but sharp-edged black humour, cracks the facade of the *bhadralok* Bengali society in Calcutta to expose the incredibly dirty going-ons in girl-running (girl-running refers to a prostitution racket that takes place under a false front). A tutorial class doubles up as a rendezvous for call-girls, the watchman functioning as a procurer in the evenings. A mother of two young girls who has pushed them into sex work, a husband who drinks and lives off his wife's earnings are actually pimps and middlemen pretending to be 'respectable' and 'honest.'

Ray also offers a critique on the system of disguised prostitution in Calcutta. The first house Somnath and his friend visit to arrange for a 'girl' to service the former's client is Mrs Ganguly. It is a typical middle-class home where we are introduced to this very attractive woman. The home reflects the middle-class status with a small piano in the sitting room and Sukumar referring to how helpful her new telephone connection has been for her business and for those who seek her services. There is a power cut and we find a candle lighting the room and Sukumar reclining on the sofa, airing himself with a hand-fan. But as she is readying herself, her husband, reportedly a clerk in the municipality, enters, completely drunk and stops her from stepping out for 'business'. He drinks off her earnings, doubles up as her pimp and decides on which assignment she will accept and which she will not. He puts his foot down, not allowing her to accompany the two men 'as she has already been out the previous two days and has a handsome appointment the following night'. He goes on to ask, 'What do we need so much money for?' The two men beat a hasty retreat.

They next visit another home, more lavishly decorated, in apparently a better locality than the former one. The lady has an Alsatian, which was a status symbol during the period

in which the film was set. She has two daughters and she has pushed both into prostitution. She seems to have redecorated the well-appointed apartment with 'two rooms, each with an attached bath' for visiting clients. She laments that a customer has taken one of her daughters to Singapore/Hong Kong and the girl jumped at it but the girl's services are being sold there.

However, when Sukumar informs her that the other daughter who is busy servicing a client in her room needs to go with them to a posh hotel, she vehemently refuses to let the girl step out to visit a client.

The third place they visit is a seedy looking coaching class where the watchman is reading from the *Ramayan*. Kawna, now named Juthika, is the sister of Somnath's friend. She symbolises a world of crumbling morals among the lower middle class on the one hand and the upper class on the other in different ways. She operates as a 'call girl' through telephonic appointments done by the watchman. She is a freelancer and visits her clients instead of the other way round. The classroom of the coaching class is used as a waiting room for girls waiting for a call. The watchman tells Sukumar that Juthika, the girl he has fixed for them, is only three months into the business but her rates have jumped from Rs 50 to Rs 250 within that short time. But she is 'invisible' and clearly belongs to the mainstream; it is clear that she comes from a lower middle class Bengali family, as does her brother, a graduate, reduced to driving a taxi.

Kawna accepts her vocation in a no-nonsense, matter-of-fact way, refusing to recognise the hero in the changed circumstances of their encounter. She denies that she is Kawna, Somnath's friend's sister and tells him repeatedly that her name is Juthika. She does not stoop to narrate a sob story to evoke his sympathy. She insists that he should not turn the taxi back to where they came from because it will be a loss for both of them. Kawna's prostitution in this film is a bribe in human form for a big contract to be gained by Somnath, the hero, while the 'taker'

of the bribe is personified in the diabetic Goenka who marries the polio-afflicted daughter of a rich businessman, showing the other side of the ugly face of corruption. The film denotes a masquerading social and moral universe. When Somnath hands her the payment, she points out that he is overpaying her but after he insists, she pockets it quietly.

Jana Aranya spells out that over time, the sex worker operates as much in the mainstream as she does in her professional ghetto of Sonarpur and Harkata Goli. So, for people living within the mainstream, it is difficult to identify a sex worker simply on the basis of where she lives. The whole city, in other words, is a 'red light area' and is no longer constrained within the limits of a marked ghetto.

All three films denote, in subtle ways, different periods in the social history of West Bengal in general and Calcutta in particular, the mainstreaming of prostitution indicating that sex work is almost as normal as being a nurse, or the wife of a pimping alcoholic or the daughters of an exploitative and greedy mother. The sex worker is neither portrayed as a victim of circumstances, nor an agency between two or more cogs in the wheel of life or even a worker belonging to an illegal, anti-social trade but as an inevitable and integral part of the ever-changing mainstream.

The 'satellite' workers who earn along the chain of sex work in red light areas are rendered redundant in mainstream prostitution. This covers the tea boys, the small *paan-bidi*-cigarette shops and flower stalls, the muscle men, the agents, the touts and the madams. This cuts down on the costs of sex work because a family member or in some cases, an entire family does the 'satellite' work!

The climax of *Jana Aranya* suggests that the hero has reduced himself to prostituting his conscience to eke out a livelihood through meagre contracts gained at the cost of procuring a woman for the contractor. He therefore, is as much, if not more, a prostitute than the prostitute he procures for his prospective clients. For example, if Kawna had not been Somnath's friend's sister, would he have suggested turning the taxi around and going back without going to the hotel for the fixed appointment? Is he sorry for the girl? Or, is he sorry for himself? The deal is done and Somnath bags the very handsome contract. But when he returns home, his body language, caught in semi-shadow as he leans against the wall near the entrance, spells out that he is not only a man defeated in the game called life but is also now, a middleman.

Only Shyam Benegal, Gulzar and a few other Indian filmmakers have dealt with prostitution as a basic socio-economic problem of a capitalist, patriarchal society. There has been no attempt, in any guise whatever, to deal with the basic problems that dodge the prostitute: medical assistance, drugs, STD and AIDS programmes, or with the decriminalisation of the prostitute. In practice, she continues to bear the brunt of punitive law-enforcement measures and legal strictures. Public opinion does not condemn the prostitute while it does condemn prostitution. She is the most visible figure, the central agent of the system and as such, the invariable target of police, judges, law-makers, the State and even social reformers.[59] The truths that ultimately comes out is that customers are seldom punished or convicted, even when they can be held guilty under the law. They repeatedly insist that 'The law isn't for people like us'[60] even in films. But if the sex worker is part of mainstream society, her 'invisibility' renders her immune from the law makers—yet never sets her free.

The sex worker is able to represent all the terms within capitalist production; she is the human labour, the object of exchange and the seller at once. She stands as worker, commodity and capitalist, and blurs the categories of bourgeois economics in the same way as she tests the boundaries of bourgeois morality. As a commodity, therefore, the prostitute both encapsulates and distorts all the classic features of bourgeois economics. This is the full nature of her threat and it is also the key to her power. But does she really enjoy power and freedom? Not really, according to these three films of Ray.

Endnotes

1. *Satyajit Ray: Artist of Social Awareness*, Buddhadeb Dasgupta, speech at the Satyajit Ray Retrospective in Calcutta reproduced in *Splice*, April 1987, p.31.
2. *Ibid.* p.32.
3. *Ibid.*
4. *Woman at the Window*, Shoma, A Chatterji, 2017, HarperCollins, Delhi.
5. *Ray's Real Women*, *The Wise One,* 19 Sept 2011.
6. *Panchali Thekey Oscar, Part II,* Devi, *op cit* pp. 176-226.
7. *Satyajit Ray's Devi: Constructing a third-world feminist critique,* Bishnupriya Ghosh, 11 May 2021
8. *Reviewing the Transition from Tradition to Modernity through Satyajit Ray's Film*, Sifat Zaman, BA dissertation at BRAC University, Dhaka, April 2012.
9. Women from the caste of barbers who pared the nails and applied *alta* (a liquid red dye prepared from the *alaktaka* flower used as a decorative by married women) to the feet of women living in the *andarmahal.*
10. Socio-cultural rituals performed by women linked mainly to birth, marriage and death.
11. Speech by Babu Girish Chandra Ghosh, 'Female Occupations in Bengal', Bengal Social Science Association, Calcutta, 30 Jan 1868, in *Sociology in India,* Centre for Sociological Research,

Calcutta, 1972, app., pp.60-61. Quoted in Footnote 5 by Sumanta Banerjee in 'Marginalization of Women's Popular Culture in Nineteenth Century Bengal' in *Recasting Women–Essays in Colonial History*, Kali for Women, Delhi, 1989, p.169.

12. *Charanamrita* (literally the nectar from the Lord's feet) which bestows immortality. Temple priests bathe the deities every day with water. This water, known as *charanamrita*, is mixed with curd and distributed to devotees, who sip some drops from their palm.
13. Interview with Sharmila Tagore for *Screen* by Shoma A Chatterji.
14. *Satyajit Ray at 100: Why Sharmila Tagore considers 'Devi' her best collaboration with the master*, Sharmila Tagore, Scroll.in, 27 Jan 2021.
15. *The Goddess: Satyajit Ray and the Myth of the Eternal Feminine,* Rafaella Britto in *The World of Apu*, A multi-lingual film magazine, 10 Jan 2018.
16. *Satyajit Ray's Devi: Constructing a third-world feminist critique* Bishnupriya Ghosh, 11 May 2021.
17. Ibid.
18. *Satyajit Ray–The Inner Eye*, Andrew Robinson, Oxford, 1989, p.150.
19. *Sahityo O Chollochitra–Satyajit Ray-er Cholochitra*, Manabendranath Saha, Prabha Prakashani, 2002, p.64.
20. Introduction to the screenplay of *Mahanagar*, Satyajit Ray, Ekkhon, 1981.
21. *Ibid.*, p.66, translation from Bengali.
22. *Cinema and Society in India and Senegal,* Akos Ostor in *Splice*, April 1987, pp.20.

23. *Modernity at Large: Cultural Dimensions of Globalization*, Arjun Appadurai, University of Minnesota Press, 1996.

24. *The City in Cinema, and Cinemas in the City: South City Mall and Locations of Display, Silhouette,* Madhuja Mukherjee, Volume VIII, 2010. p.94.

25. *Mrinal Sen's Calcutta,* Ghosh, Swapan Kumar, *Special Effects, The Indian Film Quarterly*, Oct-Dec, 1993, p.18.

26. *German Ideology*, Marx and Engels, 1976, Lawrence and Wishart, London.

27. *Patriarchy and Women's Oppression: An Examination of Marx and Engels,* Manoshi Mitra in Susheela Kaushik (ed.) *Women's Oppression – Patterns and Perspectives*, 1985, Shakti Books, Delhi, pp.26-27.

28. *Looking Again at Engel's Origin of Family*, R Delmar in J Mitchell and A Oakley, *The Rights and Wrongs of Women*, 1976, Penguin, p.287.

29. *Class in a Capitalist Society*, Westergard and Resler (1976) Penguin, Harmondsworth, quoted by Paul, Suguna in 'The Economics of Women's Oppression' in Susheela Kaushik (ed.) *Women's Oppression – Patterns and Perspectives,* Shakti Books, Delhi, p.37.

30. *Ibid.* pp.37-38.

31. Zillah R Eisenstein (ed.) *Patriarchy and the Case for Socialist Feminism*, 1979, Monthly Review Press, New York, p.22.

32. *The Cinema of Satyajit Ray-Between Tradition and Modernity,* Darius Cooper, Cambridge University Press, Cambridge, 2000, p.97.

33. *Ray's Men and Women,* Chidananda Dasgupta, Montage Magazine.

34. Andrew Robinson, op cit.

35. *Ibid.*

36. *The Broken Nest* (*Nastaneer*), Rabindranath Tagore: trans. Mary M Lago and Supriya Bari, Macmillan India, 1973, p.1.

37. Chidananda Dasgupta: *op cit*, pp. 36-37.

38. Rabindranath Tagore's letter to Murari Bhaduri, 1929. Cited in Arun Kumar Roy, *Rabindranath O Chalachitra*, Calcutta, 1986.

39. *Another Cinema for Another Society*, Gaston Roberge, Seagull Books, Calcutta.

40. *Ibid.*

41. *Charulata Prasange,* Satyajit Ray in *Parichay*, Calcutta, 1964. Collected in Satyajit Ray's *Bishay Chalachitra* (Bengali). *Paan* (betel leaf) is a heart-shaped leaf of a plant that only in a shade built outdoors. Taken by Indians mainly after meals, it is said to have digestive qualities. Earlier, it was a sort of addiction with a dash of tobacco added to give it a special 'kick.' To make it delectable, spces like pieces of betel nut, aniseed, cardamom, cinnamon, etc. are placed on it, folded into a triangle and 'pinned' with a clove. The preparation of *paan* was once considered an art form to be taught by mothers to young girls before they got married. The ingredients of the finished *paan* were kept in a special box which itself is a quaint *obet d' art,* much sought after by collectors. The entire social structure that revolved around the *paan* has all but disappeared in West Bengal in general except among old women in villages and in small towns. There is a superstition that if a *paan* is directly put into somebody's mouth, the two people involved in this act will not meet each other at the time of the other's death.

42. *Ibid.*

43. *Ibid.* Amitabha Chattopadhyay: pp. 82-148

44. *Ibid.* Chidananda Dasgupta: *The Cinema of Sayajit Ray*, p.39.

45. *Ibid.* Ray's Interview to Srinjoy Choudhury of *The Telegraph*, 1 May 1992, p.1.

46. *Ibid.* Chidananda Dasgupta, p.37.

47. *Satyajit Ray–Twenty-Five Films*, National Film Development Corporation of India, Mumbai, 1985-86, p.13

48. In one of his last interviews before he passed away, Ray told Srinjoy Choudhury of *The Telegraph* (1 May 1992) Arts supplement p.II: 'The freeze-framing of the final shot of the film was a last-minute decision. I had originally planned to have Bhupati slowly enter Charulata's room, with the servant slowly leaving. Then I realised that reconciliation would not be easy—the wish to reconcile is there, but that is not enough. Too much has happened before. The freeze frame is the visual equivalent. It tries to show that a reconciliation will take time.'

49. *Bengali Film Debates–The Literary Liaison Revisited* in *Journal of the Moving Image*, Moinak Biswas, Autumn 1999, No.1, (Department of Film Studies, Jadavpur University, Calcutta,) p.10.

50. *Ibid.*

51. *Bouthaan* is an outdated, turn-of-the-century form of address the husband's younger brother used for an older brother's wife. With time, this has been truncated and modernised to *Boudi.* The word *bou* in Bengali, means both 'wife' and 'daughter-in-law'. The added *thaan* refers to a female who is senior either in terms of chronological age, or relationship (wife of an older brother) or both. The 'connotative' function of this address is that the minute it is used as a direct form of address, it suggests a sweet relationship between the one that uses it (the husband's younger brother) and the one it is used on (his older brother's wife.) This relationship has no similarity with the bonding that exists between a blood brother and sister, or between first cousins. Nor does it have the physical intimacy between a

husband and his wife. It is a relationship which, when probed, defies definition and it is this 'unrecognisable' area lying between the defined and the ambiguous, and the possibilities that lie therein, that both Tagore and Ray sought in their own different ways and language to bring to light. Manisha Roy's *Bengali Women*, published in 1972, gives a detailed account of the social construction of sex roles in upper middle-class Bengali society.

52. Moinak Biswas, op. cit. p.11.

53. *Svarnalata* (1873), was the first domestic novel in Bengali written by Taraknath Ganguli (1845-91). The novel is known for its genuine realism. The characters are drawn directly from life. There is no influence of Bankim Chandra Chatterjee, either in technique or in style. Ganguli wrote three stories and two more novels, the materials of which also appear to have come mainly from his own experience. He was a medical doctor in government service. (Source: Sukumar Sen, p. 217.)

54. In Tagore's *Nastaneer*, Charu's topic was *Kalitala*—a nostalgic piece on the Kali temple in her village. Ray changes it to a nostalgic journey into the village of her childhood. One is not sure why Ray introduced this change but it could perhaps be because Ray, from the Brahmo Samaj himself, wished to invest her writing with a more secular (Kali Temple having obvious Hindu connotations) and universal base. Memories of childhood are a universal theme. For an international audience, it would definitely have an edge over memories of a Kali Temple.

55. Moinak Biswas, op.cit.

56. Ibid.

57. Chidananda Dasgupta, op.cit. n.xlix, p.77. Dasgupta gives a brilliant description of this scene where Charu's reflective face is superimposed with images from her childhood, images that

rock in counterpoint to the lateral movement of her face as she rocks gently on the swing. The design of the movement not only maintains the continuity of her swinging throughout the visions that are passing through her mind, but parallels the rhythm of the process through which she arrives at a sure idea of what she wants to write. The scene is an example of Ray's mastery over rhythm, arising exactly from the action and revealing its exact meaning without the help of words.

58. *The Prostitution Question(s): (Female) Agency, Sexuality and Work* Rajeswari Sunder Rajan in Ratna Kapur (ed.) *Feminist Terrains in Legal Domains: Interdisciplinary Essays on Women and Law in India,* Kali for Women, Delhi, 1996, p.123.
59. *Redefining Prostitution*, Syed Zubair Ahmed, *The Times of India*, 27 Jan 1993.
60. *Sisters of The Night,* Karyn Kay in Bill Nichols (ed.) *Movies and Methods,* Vol.I, 1993, Seagull Books, Calcutta, p.193.

AN ODE TO RAY'S MUSIC

THE CONCISE OXFORD Dictionary defines music as 'the art of combining vocal or instrumental sounds (or both) to produce beauty of form, harmony, and expression of concepts of music.' According to Wikipedia, 'Music is one of the universal cultural aspects of all human societies...The creation, performance, significance, and even the definition of music varies according to culture and social context.'

Examined closely, both these definitions fit smoothly into Satyajit Ray as the only filmmaker other than Charlie Chaplin who took complete charge of creating the music for his films from the time he made *Teen Kanya* (1960) till his last film. His son Sandip Ray, a filmmaker in his own right, depends on his father's theme music in his own films and has gone on record to say this. In celebration of the centenary of Satyajit Ray, one of the ten best directors in world cinema, it is relevant to look deeply into the way Ray looked at, treated, created, composed and directed the music in his films.

Ray once observed:

> Films and music have so much in common. Both unfold over a period of time; both are concerned with pace and rhythm and contrast; both can be described in terms of mood—sad, cheerful, pensive, boisterous, tragic and jubilant. But this resemblance applies only to Western classical music. Since our music is improvised, its pattern and duration are flexible…Also, the structure of Indian music is decorative, not dramatic.[1]

Debojyoti Misra, internationally renowned music composer and director who was introduced to the world of music by his erudite father at the tender age of three, says, 'I was the main violinist in *Ghare Baire.* I observed while working with this great man that he combined within the same persona, the two roles of a music composer and a music director.' Elaborating on the difference between the two, he says, 'If we take the example of *Pather Panchali*, Pandit Ravi Shankar composed the musical score but Ray directed the music. This means that while the music composer creates the music, the

positioning, the visualisation, the placing and the holistic perspective of the audio-visual orchestration is given by the music director, in this case, Ray.'

Ray asked some of the most celebrated among Indian musicians to compose the music for his first few films such as Pandit Ravi Shankar for the *Apu Trilogy* and *Parash Pathar* (1958) and Ustad Vilayat Khan for *Jalsaghar* (The Music Room, 1958). For this film, Ray also used sitar and surbahar exponents Imrat Khan and Wahid Ali Khan alongside Ustad Bismillah Khan roped in for the *shehnai*. Begum Akhtar portrayed the role of Durgabai, a singer. He chose Ali Akbar Khan for *Devi* (1960).

Ray had come to understand that firstly, the very famous music scholars he worked with for his first few films were too busy to give him the kind of time and space he demanded. Secondly, professional musicians would never bend their talents or compromise even a bit with the demands of a film. Last, but not the least, he could feel an undercurrent of resentment because they were being guided and controlled by a person who knew much less about music than they did. So, it was a clash between two creative persons from two different fields: one, a master in music knowing little about cinema and the other, a filmmaker who had very clear ideas of what music exactly he wanted for which film. Ray had his own creative ideas about what the music should be in his film and he knew that he could not do this with other people's ideas dominated more by their music and less by the subject/film for which they are composing the music.

Ray decided to take the baton from *Teen Kanya* (1960) comprised of three short stories adapted from Rabindranath Tagore. For his documentary *The Inner Eye* on his artistic guru Binode Behari Mukhopadhyay who was slowly going blind even as the film was being shot, Ray used a composition by the late Nikhil Ranjan Banerjee as the theme music for the film. He created theme music for every film of his and this became so much a part of his 'signature' that when one of these play on television before a commercial or show that has no link with Ray, we can immediately identify it with Ray and his film even if we may not be able to pinpoint the film.

'I began to love music long before I began to love cinema,' he would often say. Mishra adds: 'His childhood nourished with the creations of Western composers gave him a very strong musical base and I think he began to think of the music right when he was writing the screenplay of his films.' Ray's Brahmo upbringing was soaked in music because even his wife Bijoya, her mother and three sisters, were extremely talented singers and they were related to the Rays. The Brahmos, a breakaway religious sect from the Brahmin community in Bengal, were progressive in their social and family lives and their women were educated, modern and encouraged to practice the liberal arts. Thus, Ray's mother could not only read English but could also translate the stories to her son in Bengali when he was little.

DEVI SHYAMA SANGEET

The music for the film *Devi* was composed by Ustad Ali Akbar Khan at a time when Satyajit Ray had not yet begun to score the music for his films. The story goes that Ray was very determined to carry out his original perspective on how the music should play so differences grew between them during the process of composition. Ray insisted on including in the film a song in praise of Kali to depict the transformation of Dayamoyee from the daughter-in-law of the Roy family to the incarnation of goddess Kali. The song is picturised on the old man whose grandson's life is believed to have been brought back from sure death to life by Dayamoyee. The scene shows a very tired Dayamoyee seated on her pedestal, stooping under the burden of being vested with the identity of Kali. As the middle-aged man sings the *Shyama Sangeet*, the camera swings from the singer seated on the steps leading to the pedestal to the long line of people moving towards the mansion to be blessed by the *charanamrit* of the 'goddess' and Dayamoyee herself.

The song begins with the line *Ebaar toke chinecchi Ma* (I have recognised you now, my mother) composed by Ramprasad. Bengal has songs composed exclusively for the worship of Shakti, known as *Shakta Padavali* or *Shyama Sangeet*, all in prayer and devotion to Kali. These form an integral, rich part of the history of Bengali literature. On another plane, down the ages, these songs have also lifted true devotees of Kali towards the fulfillment of their goal—to be able to touch and reach their goddess. These songs are believed to pull the goddess closer towards her devotee. *Shyama Sangeet* songs have been composed and set to tune by Kali devotees who have attained a high level of spiritual awakening. They are said to be completely spontaneous outpourings.

These songs are sung in the presence of Kali or Shyama, and even in her absence to invoke her 'presence' in spirit. In course of time, *Shyama Sangeet* has become in inseparable part of Kali worship as it evolved into a cultural and spiritual treasure of Bengali music and literature. Most of these songs are qualified by an attempt to bring Kali into the mainstream or bring the universal mother into the home of the Kali devotee as if she is his own mother and through this, basking in the happiness of spiritual fulfillment. This song is said to have been picked from the numerous compositions by Sadhak Ramprasad and is popularly known as *Prosadi Sangeet*.

Ramprasad Sen (Kaviranjan) was born in a village called Kumarhatta, a place around twenty kilometres from Kolkata up the Hooghly river. The date of his birth is not certain but some sources trace it to 1723.[2] However, this could be incorrect because another source states that when he arrived in Calcutta sometime around 1730, he was eighteen years old.[3] He landed the job of an accounts clerk in the office of a Bengali *diwan* or estate manager. He was a devotee of Kali from a tender age, writing poems dedicated to Kali in his account books. His songs were distinctive in their originality because they brought Kali down from her inaccessible high altar to the level of a human being. In so doing, through his compositions, he could demystify Kali by domesticating her and thereby stripping her of the aura of godliness and fear. In other words, he attempted to narrow down the distance between Kali and her devotees by converting the relationship between the two to one of mother and son, or in a bolder way, turning the devotee into a 'devourer' of the goddess. Contrary to common expectations, people liked this unique approach towards the goddess and were deeply influenced by the spirit of the compositions.

If in one composition Ramprasad reduces himself to an ideal child of the goddess, in another, he personifies Kali as the Great Mother with the people of the world being her children who she plays with as if they are toys. Like one does with playthings, at times she pampers them while at others, she rejects and discards them, in keeping with her role of creator and destroyer at the same time. But human beings, says Ramprasad, "are not inanimate objects, so just as children respond to their mother's behaviour with them, her 'children' too respond with joy when they are pampered and simper when they are discarded".

GOOPY GAYEN BAGHA BAYEN DRUMS

Ray was brought up in a progressive ambience. This finds reflection both in his women characters and in the music he composed. If *Goopy Gayen Bagha Bayen* is taken to be a typical example, it is layered with music drawn from across many schools of music in the country and the world.

For *Goopy Gayen Bagha Bayen*, Ray composed all his scores following Occidental musical notes. Then, he discovered that musicians in Bengal were not familiar with western notations at all. It took them time to convert the notations to Indian, especially Bengali ones. So, Ray learnt and started composing in Bengali notations. The magical results can be heard till today. After he decided to be his own composer and music director, he often wrote the lyrics too.

During the initial stages of his career, Ray used to compose the tunes on piano. For the background scores, he generally used violins, cellos and double bass guitars, not the Indian bamboo flute. He also had a great love for several Indian percussions and superbly used the timpani, a western drum, on some occasions.

'One of the outstanding features of the songs of *Goopy Gayen Bagha Bayen* are the lyrics that children and adults would equally enjoy and the use of drums focused on the drummer of the duo Bagha while Goopy stuck to vocals,' explains Mishra, who can seamlessly play on a whole lot of instruments having trained in the violin under Sisir Kona Dhar Choudhury and begun working and training under the great Salil Chowdhury from the time he was eighteen years old.

This film also stands out because he picked on a relatively lesser known but trained classical singer Anup Ghosal who had a PhD in music, to give voice for the songs lip-synced by Tapen Chatterjee, also a new find portraying Goopy. There are ten songs in the film and the lyrics are all penned by Ray himself. He picked up a four-page story written by his grandfather, the late Upendrakishore Roy Choudhury, and then expanded it into a full-length feature film.

He used some Carnatic tunes for some of the songs that vested these numbers with a slight comic tone as the film was entertaining and also carried subtle political messages against dictatorship, corruption in high places and the significance of silence. Songs like *Dekho re noyon mele* (Just open your eyes and see), or *Ek je chhilo raja* (Once there was a king) are timeless among Bengali music and cinema fans till today.

On the other hand, the rhymes recited by the King of Ghosts (Bhooter Raja) said to be a designedly distorted version, recorded in Ray's voice, was not sung but had wonderful music to string the two together which, perhaps, may be interpreted as Ray's own creation of rap and its introduction into Indian cinema much before rap was officially born in Africa around the 1980s mainly as a form of poetry recited to musical beats and notes. Rap expresses different emotions but it is popularly identified with protest, rebellion, resistance, mainly coming from marginalised pockets of people performed with vigorous and vibrant body movement trying to involve the audience to the act.

Rapping (also rhyming, spitting, emceeing) is a musical form of vocal delivery that incorporates 'rhyme, rhythmic speech and street vernacular,' performed or chanted in a variety of ways, usually over a backing beat or musical accompaniment and this is clearly borne out in the performance of the King of Ghosts in this film.

HIRAK RAJAR DESHE FOLK MUSIC

This 1980 film is like a sequel to *Goopy Gayen Bagha Bayen* but the only thing common between the two is the presence of Goopy and Bagha with their magical powers. They arrive on the invitation of the king of Halla for a function and find that he is an absolute dictator who not only makes complete slaves of his subjects but also 'brainwashes' them through an invention by the resident scientist. The unique feature of the film is that the entire dialogue was written in rhyme form by Ray himself. It is fascinating to discover this in a fairy tale, surrealistic film which children and adults have loved for different reasons.

The opening frames take us back to Goopy and Bagha to impart continuity and as a recap for the audience where Goopy sings *Mora dujo nayera jarja mai,* establishing that their marriage to the two daughters of the king of Shundi is now ten years old and they are fed up of their very lazy life stripped of any sign of adventure. We are also offered a glimpse

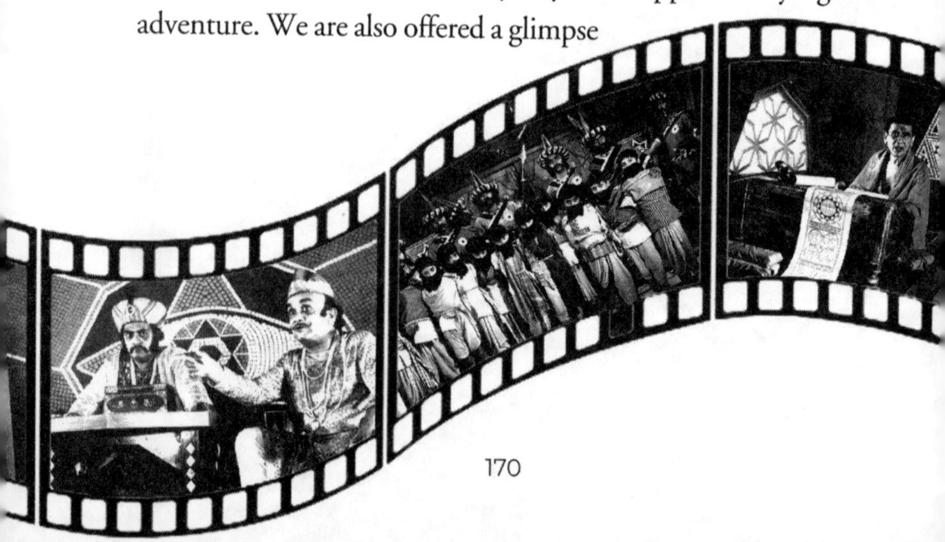

of the now white-haired king of Shundi who suggests they go to attend an important ceremony in the land ruled over by the king of Halla.

But the USP of the film lies in a song *Kotoi rongo dekhi duniaye* (How many colours do we see in this world!) filled with biting satire, sung by a doddering old musician who has been commanded not to sing. This small role was played by Robin Majumdar who was a noted singing hero of old Bengali films but did not work any more. That is just half the story. Who gave the voice to this actor? He was one of the biggest authorities on folk music in Bengal. His name was Amar Pal and Ray chose him because the song had a folk tune and he knew no one would do justice to it the way Amar Pal would. His faith was proven because this song became a thumping hit with music lovers across West Bengal. Pal was hesitant to sing for Ray as he doubted if he would be able to do justice to the song the way Ray had conceived it. The last two lines went: *Dekh valo jone roilo vanga ghore, Mondo je se singhasone chore* 'Look how the good man lives in a broken home/While the evil man climbs on the throne,' which rings the death knell for the singer in the film. Though Pal was famous for his incredible command over folk music in Bengal—both its history and his performance—he was nervous while lending his voice in a Ray film despite having lent his voice to many other filmmakers too, such as Tapan Sinha, Debaki Bose, Arundhati Devi and Pijush Bose. Afterwards, he cherished the memory of this song, that was recorded in a single take. This song is repeated towards the end when the same singer belts out the song and the king of

Halla turns speechless with anger.

The other song *Paaye podi baagh Mama* (Oh Tiger Uncle, we fall at your feet) that turned out to be a hit with video clips running on YouTube is the one Goopy sings when they are trapped in the tiger's den and scared to death. They have been pushed into the cell to steal the diamonds. The song is set to music drawn from Karnataka classical strains which lends the mood of the comic and the ironical. The tiger is mesmerised by their singing and they make their escape without getting caught. The scene evokes fun instead of fear in the audience.

The lyrics of the song numbers in *Hirak Rajar Deshe* (Kingdom of Diamonds) ended up being more meaningful than its tune, as the mood is a carryover from *Goopy Gayen Bagha Bayen.*

MONIHARA MYSTERIOUS THEMES

In the second of the triple-story film *Teen Kanya* which Ray made in celebration of Tagore's centenary, we watch the loneliness of Monimalika, the wife of the rich jute merchant. They are childless and she is obsessed with jewellery, both buying and possessing it. In the initial days of her marriage, she sings a sad song alone, facing the window of her room, the lace curtains fluttering in the breeze. The first line of the song, *Baaje koruno shure*[4] (It plays a very sad tune) becomes the mysterious theme music of the film used in a slightly innovative variation by Ray. Phanibhushan, her husband, enters but waits at the door, a shadowy figure, then enters the room after the song ends. He takes a small box out of his pocket and gifts it to Monimalika. It is a pair of ear-rings. She at once takes them out of the box, moves towards the mirror on the dresser and begins to put them on. We never hear her sing again and Phanibhushan has no ear for music at all.

CHARULATA ON VIOLIN AND QUINTET

Is *Charulata* designed on the lines of a Mozart[5] composition? Musically, Ray referred to *Charulata* as his string quintet with Charu as first violin, Amal as second violin, Bhupati as cello, that is the three dominant characters. Umapada and Mandakini are referred to as the two violas who, though not dominant, are still essential characters for the quintet. It is a beautiful musical simile.[6] Western classical music critic Kishore Chatterjee takes this argument further and insists that Ray structured the characters along the orchestration and composition of a specific and very original composition of the great Austrian composer, Wolfgang Amadeus Mozart.[7] Art historian Partha Mitter revealed to us something of Ray's Mozartian sensibility. He writes: 'Ray spoke vividly of how Mozart (and Verdi) had solved the problem of treating a dramatic situation musically through the interplay of multiple, concurrent vocal parts. What I did not realise then was the profoundly musical and even operative nature of Ray's own sensibility.'[8]

Charulata is like a particular chamber composition of Mozart. It cannot be placed on par with a 'symphony' composition because it has just five characters like a quintet has five instruments. Symphony music is composed of many musical instruments of varied kinds, creating a completely different kind of 'grandeur' in terms of music. Chamber compositions are subtle and understated. In *Charulata*, the emotions are soft, low-key, yet clear and articulate. Mozart's compositions are known for their expressions of exuberance, joy and a sense of complacence, of pleasure. Mozart also composed musical pieces that expressed sorrow and pathos but they were fewer in number. In his short 36-year-old life, Mozart created 626 musical compositions. Interestingly however, all his compositions that were 'sad' go under the label of 'String Quintet in G-Minor.' *Charulata* is a fine, smooth fusion of the happy and the sad, of the joy of love and the sorrow of parting, of the spontaneous thrill of having discovered love, followed by the hurt of betrayal. The sorrow and pathos of parting and of loneliness, is the dominant emotion in the film.

The entire structure of *Charulata* bears a striking resemblance to Mozart's 'G-Minor String Quintet, K.516' according to Kishore Chatterjee.[9] Mozart composed only three major pieces in the G-Minor scale, of which two are 'symphonies' and one is a 'chamber music' piece. Mozart felt sadness and pathos were ideally created in the G-Minor scale. The two symphonies he composed in G-Minor cannot be linked here because of its use of more than five instruments. K.516 is the sole chamber piece Mozart composed in which pathos is the only emotion that reigns from beginning to end. The spirit of *Charulata* and the emotional fluctuations the five characters go through is contained within this Mozart composition. All incidents in the story—the drama, the conflict, the climax—are confined to these five characters alone.

Umapada and Mandakini appear to be in the background, yet both are crucial to the events and to the changes brought about in the lives of the other three. Umapada betrays the trust his brother-in-law places in him. It shocks Bhupati into realising that never mind how close one thinks people are, they are not beyond betraying one's trust. Amal realises that he too has betrayed Bhupati in a different way. When Amal goes away, it is Charu who feels betrayed by the two men in her life—Bhupati, her husband, who has 'sentenced' her to a life of loneliness, and Amal, who ran away like a coward when he realised that their relationship was treading on dangerous ground. Mandakini, Umapada's simple wife, offers a counterpoint to Charu, who finds in her a rival for Amal's attentions. When the two go away, followed by Amal, they trigger off a chain of apparently simple events in Charu and Bhupati's life that has repercussions deeper than are immediately apparent.

The sound of the violin is sensitive, soft and has an undercurrent of sweet pathos in it. So, Amal and Charu are the two 'violins' in this String Quintet. They are two sensitive, soft and romantic human beings. The cello, on the other hand has a serious, grave and sombre tone. It also has an aura of

indifference. Bhupati thus represents the cello.

The two violas in the Mozart quintet offer background support, instruments that are not directly involved in creating the final composition, but lend themselves critically to the three major instruments to help reach the climactic notes in the entire piece. That is why it can be said that Umapada and his wife Mandakini symbolise the two violas in the 'Mozart composition' that defines *Charulata*. The violas intensify the mood of sorrow and pathos created by the two violins.

The structure of this particular Mozart composition, which Ray reportedly listened to over and over again since he was a young man, became so much a part of him that it influenced his thinking when he designed the script for *Charulata* and fleshed out the five characters in the film. Inspired by Mozart's 'abstract choreography of sounds' in this piece, Ray converted this to a 'choreography of human bodies' because the movements of the characters, the composition of each frame in the film, the pacing and the rhythm of their entries and exits into and from these frames, are reminiscent of the 'musical movements' of the five different string instruments in K.516, a composition that dates to the last stages of his life. Thus, it is tinged with the pathos and the melancholy drawn from Mozart's entire life, never mind its brief span. Ray transformed the 'listening musical choreography' of Mozart into a 'visual choreography' of cinema, proving that one element of art, music, can quite smoothly be transported into another form, cinema, with equal finesse and great emotional impact.

The music of *Charulata* has become iconic in the history

of music in world cinema. Ray picked up the main tune from a famous Tagore number *Momo chittey niti rittey ke je naachey* (Someone dances inside my heart). as the theme music and extended it into a long, melodious and very subtle signature tune that creates the effect of cascading water like a very slow undercurrent throughout the film. The tune gets embedded into the film and plants itself in the minds of the audience as well. The words of the song or the song itself are never articulated throughout the film. Even in the opening scene when Charu picks out a book by Bankim Chandra Chattopadhyay, she begins to hum 'Bankim Bankim' in a musical chant repeatedly which makes an intriguing impact focussing on her loneliness.

Later, when Charu is swinging on the swing in their unkempt garden, she begins to slowly render the Tagore number *Phoole phoole dhole dhole bayukee bamridu baaye* (A touch of sweetness in the breeze that softly cradles buds today).

ASHANI SANKET ON OMINOUS MELODY AND DRUMS

Ashani Sanket, Ray's second feature film in colour, explored the man-made 1943 Bengal famine that took the lives of five million people. What makes the film a classic is its music and soundtrack. The opening frames are backed by the sound of drumbeats that have an ominous tone. The same kind of music is repeated towards the end when disaster and tragedy have struck the village, impacting heavily on the value systems of its entire population. There are spaces of silence too at different points of the film. The soundtrack gives the rural backdrop an identity.

There is a moment when it is raining and suddenly, the loud sound of war planes can be heard; Chhutki and Ananga look skywards while returning from the forest after collecting wild potatoes for lunch. They probably sight the planes which are off frame.

GHARE BAIRE TAGORE AND RAY

The musical score of *Ghare Baire (The Home and the World),* adapted as a period piece from a novelette by Rabindranath Tagore, follows the changing moods and ambience of the film's politically powerful backdrop. Originally published in Bengali (as *Ghare Baire*) in 1915, it was later translated and published in English by the author's nephew Surendranath Tagore (with active cooperation from the author himself) in 1919. The Bengali original was published two years after the author was awarded the Nobel Prize for Literature and the same year in which he received a knighthood from King George V of England—an accolade he renounced in 1919 in protest against the Jallianwala Bagh massacre in Punjab.

The Home and the World did not have an easy passage. Satyajit Ray had originally planned to adapt Tagore's novel—written in the form of a diary with three voices—way back in 1948. His interest in the project waxed and waned in the years after. Shooting in Calcutta began in December 1982. But the film could only be completed due to Ray's prolonged illness till May 1984, just in time for the Cannes Festival.

Ray's comment on this film goes like this:

> *The Home and the World* is a triangular love story. The husband is really Tagore. There are essays by Tagore on this terrorist movement, and some of the things he wrote, even exact sentences, are put into the mouth of the main character, Nikhil. He represents Tagore's attitude to the

> terrorist movement and its ultimate futility. It is a very valid viewpoint and very rational. It was really a middle-class movement with no connection to the lower strata of society at all. So ultimately, it just fizzled out, and in other cases it turned into very violent riots between Hindus and Muslims. Tagore withdrew from the movement and came out with the essays and then, four or five years later, in 1912, he produced this novel.

There are three songs in the film. Of these, two are patriotic and one is a very teasing kind of song. The first song is written and composed by Tagore which goes *Bidhir bandhon kaatbe tumi emon Shaktimaan* (You are powerful enough to break the bond of destiny) which tends to raise the awareness of the masses towards India's struggle for freedom. The second song conveys the same mood: *Chawl re chawl shob bharato shontan matribhoomi kore ahwan* (Oh children of India, Let us all march becauase motherland is calling us). Both these songs carry the ambience and mood of patriotic songs composed and written by the revolutionary poet Kazi Nazrul Islam, though the second song was composed by Tagore's brother, Jyotirindranath Tagore. The third song *Bujhte nari nari kee chaye* (I cannot understand what a woman wants) was written by Akshay Kumar Boral and its music was composed by Rabindranath Tagore. It was a romantic song sung teasingly by Sandip to take a poke at Bimala, who is very attracted to him.

Ray worked magic by using the beautiful tune minus the lyrics of a famous Tagore number that went *Eki anando bonney purno prano praneshohi,* slowing down the melody and expanding it through purely instrumental music to mark Bimala's stepping out from the inner sanctum of the palace to the outer wing to meet Sandip, a radical step taken by a housewife of a landlord's family during the period of the film. The repeated chanting of *Bande mataram* initiated by Sandip in the film does not gain the kind of popularity he had expected as the very poor Muslim traders of the village did not take kindly to his sermonising, which went totally against their livelihood interests. But Bimala was enchanted, not because it was a patriotic chant but because it was being chanted by Sandip. But this same chant is chanted at the end of the opening frames in a chorus against the music of what almost sounds like the echoes of the fire in the Visalakshi temple in the distance which we see behind Bimala's face in the distance when the film opens.

The story goes that Ray's passion for Western classical music was perhaps born when as a boy of nine, he heard a gramophone record play Beethoven's *Violin Concerto* in the

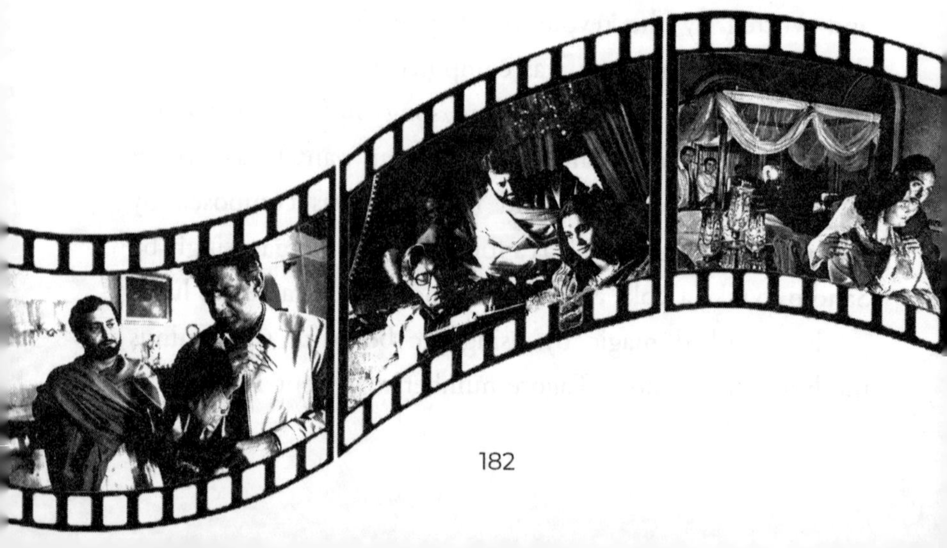

home of his mother's brother. This particular record and its music made such a deep impact on this small boy that he grasped whatever he could: books, notes, papers, records on Western classical music with of course, a special love for Beethoven. His family had gifted him with a small gramophone and he considered it one of the best gifts during his boyhood. His being essentially a loner who thought more than he played, and drew and sketched and listened to music much more than he did anything else drove him to a devoted listener of music. Perhaps, this was a precursor to his creating and directing music for his own films later on. Over his long career, Ray made thirty-six films (twenty-nine feature films, five documentaries and two short films), and provided music for as many as thirty of them.

It may come as a surprise that Ray had no formal training in any kind of music—Western classical, Hindustani classical or even Bengali songs such as those composed by Tagore. He learnt everything by ear and even composed by listening to himself humming or whistling a note and then asking his musicians to put it to music. But he taught himself the piano which still stands in his study as a slice of memory. On top of this piano stood a bust of the composer Mozart. But when it came to film music, he regarded the Russian composer Sergei Prokofiev as his guru.

Ray took every opportunity to learn about and listen to as much of Western classical music as possible during his two-year stay in Santiniketan. This was possible because of the encouragement he got from a German-Jewish professor of

English in Viswa Bharati who had an enviable collection of Western Classical composers' works in records. He threw this treasure open for Ray to listen to as many times as he wanted. Mishra recollects an anecdote about how Ray and his wife Bijoya—a very talented singer in her own right—would often listen to the compositions of Bach and Haydn on Radio Berlin during World War II. Few are aware that once Ray had got an offer from BBC to make a documentary on Mozart's opera *Don Giovanni* but he could not accept it. This is an indicator of how the news of his command over Western Classical music and composers had reached far and wide quite early.

The late Dinkar Kaushik, one of Ray's oldest friends from his days at Santiniketan, who later headed Kala Bhavan, said that Ray once toyed with the idea of making a documentary on Pandit Ravi Shankar in 1948, much before the latter became an internationally renowned celebrity.

> He asked me to get back a sketchbook of his from Ravi Shankar from Delhi. When I thumbed through its pages, its contents amazed me. It was filled with close-up sketches of Ravi Shankar at his sitar, done from every imaginable angle, marking fade-outs, highlights, crisscross marks for shootings, detailed studies of the maestro's hands, fingers, everything. It was a collage of work that did not merely inspire, but evoked instant emotional response.[10]

Regrettably, Ray never got down making that documentary. But a few years ago, HarperCollins India brought out a hard copy of Ray's original script for the film which never got made.

Ray was very fond of Indian classical music, Rabindra Sangeet and Bengali folk music, all of which he used extensively in his films. But what is not widely known is that he was vastly more knowledgeable in and passionate about Western classical music.

Filmmaker Utpalendu Chakrabarty made a documentary film produced by NFDC called *The Music of Satyajit Ray* in 1984. The film was cast on an OTT platform last year in celebration of Ray's ninety-ninth birth anniversary. The documentary moves between the studio where Ray and his orchestra are composing background score for his then-upcoming film *Ghare Baire*, and his home, where he sits in front of a Roland piano, either striking musical notes on his Roland piano or using his pen to write down notations. He is perhaps one of the only filmmakers of his time who could both, read and write notations of Western classical music.

As the camera focuses on Ray speaking about the musical talent across his family spread across four generations including his mother, Suprabha Roy, who had also cut a record of her song, we see the camera pan across through old monochrome photographs of his forefathers. This throws up a subtle pointer to Ray's being born into music in a manner of speaking as much as his being born into creative art like drawing and painting, prints and fonts and creative writing. The narrative cuts back and forth with clips from Ray's films that are further enriched by his music interspersed with Ray composing at home and in the studios with his entire orchestra.

Ray had an uncanny ear for silence too. His film *Pratidwandi* either has long tracks of silence as the camera keeps following the protagonist Siddhartha Choudhury, the soundtrack is quite silent filled with ambient sounds such as the cry of birds or moving vehicles. Sometimes, the soundtrack is silent even when we find public vehicles moving on the roads and that is perhaps recorded from the hero Siddhartha's perspective where he is absent-minded even when he is walking and not taking note of either the visuals or the sounds that surround him.

Ray also scored the music for documentaries like *Glimpses of West Bengal*, *Gangasagar Mela* and *Darjeeling: Himalayan Fantasy* directed by Bansi Chandragupta, *House that Never Dies* by Tony Meyer, *Max Mueller* by John Thiele, and *Quest of Health* by Harisadhan Dasgupta. Among feature films of other directors, Ray is credited for the music of *Baksa Badal* (Director: Nityananda Datta), *Shakespeare Wallah* (Director: James Ivory) and *Fatikchand* (Director: Sandip Ray) as also for Sandip's TV serials like *Satyajit Ray Presents (Part I and II).*

As if all this is not enough, Chunibala who, at 75, portrayed the iconic doddering old Indir Thakrun in Ray's *Pather Panchali*, asked Ray if he would like to hear her sing a particular song. She sang beautifully and Ray was taken aback. This song, in Chunibala's voice, was used in the film and Ray was amazed with her performance and her music. The actress, who had done two silent films when she was young, died before *Pather Panchali* was released.

The song went thus: *Hori din to gelo sondhya holo paar koro amaare* meaning, 'God, the day has passed on, it is evening now, help me cross to the other side.' This philosophical number, was replayed on the soundtrack when little Apu is following her hearse to the crematorium after her death in the film.

Endnotes

1. Elizabeth U Harding, *Kali-The Black Goddess of Dakshineswar*, 1998, Motilal Banarsidass Publishers, Delhi, p. 215.
2. Sumanta Banerjee: 'The Changing Role of Kali' in *Logic in a Popular Form – Essays on Popular Religion in Bengal*, Seagull Books, Calcutta, 2002, p. 52.
3. *Baaje karuno shurey*, a Tagore composition, was sung by Kanika Bandyopadhyay during Tagore's birth centenary celebrations in 1961. The original Tamil version *Needu charanamule* was sung by Swagatalakshmi Dasgupta (1999). According to the *Sangeeta Sudha*, the song was composed by Thyagaraja and its tune is set to Raga *Simhendra Madhyam*. Tagore picked up Carnatic music from Savithri Krishnan, (a girl who became a student at Viswa Bharati) to compose some of his most well-known songs. Tagore had discovered her at Adyar when she was 14 years old. *Source:* Dipankar Dasgupta in *Tagore, Savithri Krishnan and Carnatic Music* http://www.boloji.com/index.cfm?md=Content&sd=Articles&ArticleID=13821http://www.boloji.com/index.cfm?md=Content&sd=Articles&ArticleID=13821 For Ray's film, Ruma Guhathakurta did the playback for Kanika Bandopadhyay who learnt to sing the song herself from Ray's wife so that the lip-sync was precise.
4. Ray's apprenticeship in Western classical music began in boyhood, with horn gramophones, borrowed discs and a

battered harmonium. At age 13, Ray and his friend Anil Gupta, began hunting for bargains in the music shops of Calcutta. Their earliest exciting discovery was the first movement of Beethoven's *Fifth Symphony*. Gupta introduced Ray to Beethoven's biography by Schindler and Donald Tovey's *Essays on Rhythm*. Soon after, they stumbled on Mozart's *Eine Kleine Nacht Music* and he lost his sleep that night. Gupta, himself a Mozart scholar, put his finger on the similarity between Mozart's compositions and the musical choreography of Ray's films. 'Nobody can improve one note of Mozart. His music is beautiful, logical, symmetrical and inevitable—like Manik's films at their best', said Gupta. (Source: Sumit Mitra: 'The Genius of Satyajit Ray' in *India Today*, 15 Feb 1983, p.73.)

5. Adi Gazder, 'In Tune with Ray–On the Set and Off it' in *The Statesman Miscellany*, 11 Oct 1992, pp.10-11.
6. Ujjal Chakrabarti: '*Charulata Keno Sangeet-er Moto–Kee Bhaabe?*' a discussion (in Bengali) between Amitabha Chatterjee and Kishore Chatterjee from Anirudhha Dhar's *Panchali Thekey Oscar*, serialised in *Sananda* (Anand Bazar Patrika Group of Publications, Calcutta, pp.100-03. (The date and month of the issue are not found in the clipping–author).
7. Quoted by Raghubir Singh in 'The River' in *Sunday*, 3-9 May 1992, p.56.
8. *Ibid.* Ujjal Chakrabarti, in *Sananda* n.6. above, p.101.
9. Kishore Chatterjee from a discussion quoted by Ujjal Chakrabarti in '*Charulata Keno Sangeet-er Moto–Kee Bhaabe?*' a discussion in Bengali.
10. This quote was used in an article in *Desh* magazine, a literary fortnightly in Bengali in a special issue on Ray following his death in June 1993.

RAY: THE MAN, THE ENIGMA

FELUDA AND HIS adventures and resolution of crimes spread across the map illustrate the genius of Ray not as a filmmaker but as a litterateur whose books for children are bestsellers that initially took his publishers by great surprise. They remain bestsellers today across two generations of readers of all ages and across languages, countries and continents.

In a recent interview with Ray's son, he elaborated on how his father became a writer of bestsellers. "When my father was a student at Kala Bhavan in Santiniketan, he had written two short stories. After all, writing ran in his blood with his grandfather, Upendra Kishore Roy Choudhury and father, Sukumar Ray being renowned authors. But those two short stories ended his affair with creative writing. But then, his close friend and poet, Subhash Mukhopadhyay persuaded him to revive the children's magazine *Sandesh*, first founded by my great-grandfather and then revived by my grandfather Sukumar Ray. Baba agreed and he, along with the celebrated poet, Subhash Mukhopadhyay, revived *Sandesh* in 1961 and the two friends edited it jointly and it soon became extremely popular among children." *Sandesh* is now edited by Sandip himself.

"Baba felt that as an editor, he also had to contribute to the creative content so he began translating the limericks of Edward Lear and the writings of Louis Carroll. But they were not his original creations so he created Professor Shanku, the mad scientist, now a literary icon, for the special Pooja Number of *Sandesh* in 1961. He created strange ideas for stories without stopping. Then, in 1965, the famous *Feluda*, the detective many say has similarities with my father, was born and became one of the most outstanding and memorable detective characters in Bengali literature. He did the illustrations himself and this added to the USP of his writings.

"I have myself made several feature films and television serials revolving around the adventures of Feluda who was an action-oriented, very intellectual detective. But looking back, the whole story of the resurrection of *Sandesh* worked like a trigger for my father's very successful career as a creative writer. But for *Sandesh*, Baba might never have switched on his writing pen, apart of course, from his film scripts and his innumerable features, articles and essays on films he wrote on the request of editors from various magazines. Volumes of Feluda's adventures remain on the top-selling list till today among children and teenagers of West Bengal."

The adventures of Feluda have also appeared in English, French, Italian and Japanese translations over the years.

FELUDA A CHARACTER AS FAMOUS AS ITS CREATOR

Feluda, a fictional detective, is identified with the person who created him—Satyajit Ray, one of the ten best filmmakers across the world, according to a cover story in *Time* magazine many summers ago. Ray began his career as a commercial artist and also worked in this capacity. He designed book covers and the logo of Nandan, a cinema complex in Calcutta. His initial steps into the creative world of fiction began with a series of detective thrillers. Nickname: Feluda. Proper name: Pradosh Mitter.

Ray created a new world for children through Feluda's adventure-filled journeys into little-known or well-known cities to solve crimes. Here, adventure forms an important segment without crime taking second place. Feluda remained confined to the pages of the printed book till Ray decided to make a film on his first adventures named *Sonar Kella* (The Golden Fort). This was published in a noted Bengali magazine with illustrations done by Ray himself. Ray also turned *Joy Baba Felunath* into a film in 1979 where Soumitra Chatterjee played Feluda, Siddhartha Chatterjee was Topshe and the iconic Santosh Dutta portrayed Jatayu.

Feluda was born in 1965, soon after Ray had honed his hidden talent with the pen through a few short sci-fi stories revolving around another famous character, Prof Shanku who has an uncanny resemblance to Prof Calculus of the Tintin stories. His first ever book, *Professor Shanku* was published by *Newscript* earlier the same year, establishing Ray as a brilliant literateur for children. Ray's first mystery-adventure on Feluda was published as *Feludar Goendagiri* (Feluda's Detecting Skills) in the children's magazine *Sandesh*, jointly edited by Ray and poet Subhash Mukhopadhyay with his aunt, Leela Majumdar, herself a noted name in children's literature joining in later. The novelette was published in three instalments. It was an instant hit.

Late Badal Bose of Ananda Publishers, involved with all of Ray's literary works, says:

> The wit, the cunning, the intelligence, the wisdom and the youth of the detective Feluda, who blends his detecting skills with a spirit of healthy adventure is unique in Bengali literature. It has never been seen before or after Feluda. As readers, we turned greedy. We began craving for a full-length novel on Feluda's adventures and mysteries. We needed to discover how Feluda would

> use his investigative skills and psychological insights in unravelling a murder or a robbery through the pages of an extended novel. Possibly, Ray understood this desire and began to serialise a full-length novel on Feluda over one year in *Sandesh*. Every reader of *Sandesh*, big or small, man, woman or child, would eagerly await the next instalment of *Badshahi Angti* (The Badshah's Ring) in the latest issue of *Sandesh*. It was a wonderful, tightly-knit novel, with full-blooded characterisations and dynamic action, all unfolded in the first person by Feluda's cousin, fan and assistant Topshe, an abbreviation for his proper name Taposh, a role repeatedly played by Siddhartha Chatterjee who is not into films today.[1]

Satyajit Ray's *Sonar Kella* (1974) introduced a six-foot charming young detective and his teenage assistant who took on a case of hypnotism and reincarnation. Many actors have portrayed the charismatic Feluda, such as Shashi Kapoor in a Hindi Doordarshan series, but Soumitra Chatterjee rightfully grabs everyone's imagination till today. Sabyasachi Chakraborty also deserves special mention for his portrayal of the Bengali detective in director Sandip Ray's Feluda films. Later, Abir Chatterjee also portrayed Feluda when Sabyasachi Chakraborty became a bit too old for Feluda and begged away from playing it. Most recently, in a web series on Feluda directed by Srijit Mukherjee, Tota Roy Choudhury has played Feluda with the action hero given a complete makeover by the director to project the typical Feluda look.

Feluda is a fictional detective who is very different from the legendary literary detectives one has known. This iconic fictional private detective is known for his remarkable flair for observation and brilliant analytical and introspective qualities along with physical attributes bordering on the fantastic. Right from its inception as a glorious milestone of Bengali literature, it garnered widespread popularity which grew all the more with films made on the character by Satyajit Ray himself, presently by his son, Sandip Ray. The adventures of Feluda have also appeared in English, French, Italian, Japanese and so on. Right from their inception as a glorious milestone of Bengali literature, the Feluda adventures garnered widespread popularity which grew all the more with films made on the character by Satyajit Ray himself, presently by his son, Sandip Ray. It has also been translated into several Indian languages like Marathi, Gujarati, Malayalam, Oriya and many more.

The titles of the Feluda adventures were very often alliterative such as *Gangtokey Gondogol, Joto Kando Kathmandu Te* and *Bombaiyer Bombetey*. As he was a trained commercial artist, Ray did vivid illustrations of the novels himself; they are very lucid and entertaining. He also designed the covers, including the graphic titles. The film also displays the massive collection of covers of the Feluda stories from time to time while Soumitra Chatterjee surprises us when he says that though he was an established actor when he played Feluda for the first time, he found himself an overnight star with the release of *Sonar Kella*. Sandip Ray adds that his father received much more fan mail from fans of Feluda than from fans of his films!

Feluda—50 Years of Ray's Detective is the first Indian biopic on a fictional character—a character that exists only in the pages of a book or a journal and not in real life. Sagnik Chatterjee's documentary, which won the National Award, showcased and analysed the unique journey spanning fifty years through fascinating interviews, invaluable illustrations, rare film and audio clips, excerpts from radio plays, audio books, comic strips et cetera, to explore how the character attained 'cult' status, and eventually became part of 'socio-cultural' existence, with admirers spanning the world.

The path-breaking documentary sheds light on the relatively lesser-known talent of Satyajit Ray as a master litterateur who illustrated and designed his books. Feluda is a walking encyclopaedia, has a miraculous memory and is a keen observer of human behaviour down to the finest nuances that enhance his powers of detection.

Feluda is arrogant but sociable. What marks him out is his adventurous spirit that takes him and his readers from Kathmandu to Kailash, from Bombay (as it was known then) to Jaisalmer in Rajasthan with his nephew-cum-assistant Topshe and a successful writer of pop detective novels with the pen name Jatayu. These are also travelogues with a twist of crime. Feluda is radically experimental in his eating habits. Feluda or Prodosh Mitter is a post-modern detective. *The Feluda Collection* still remains among the top-selling books for growing and adolescent children.

In the beginning, the character of Feluda as described

and illustrated by Ray, seemed to be fleshed out as an autobiographical sketch of Ray himself. But over time, Feluda outgrew his creator and assumed an independent identity. Chatterjee recalls:

> Once, scriptwriter Shama Zaidi told me a strange story. She said that during the making of *Shatranj Ke Khiladi*, she was travelling in a train from Delhi to Lucknow along with Satyajit Ray. His height drew the attention of some of the passengers and one of them asked Ms Zaidi about this tall gentleman who looked so familiar. When she told them that this was Satyajit Ray, the man immediately said, 'Oh! This means the writer who writes books for children, right.' I was thrilled because till then, I had no clue that his Feluda stories had travelled beyond Bengal and already had a pan-India identity. He was no less famous as a writer than he was as a great filmmaker. Perhaps, it was then that the seeds of this film were sown in me.
>
> I first came across documents related to Feluda in Satyajit Ray's personal library. It was around 2006/2007 during assisting Sandip Ray in *Tintorettor Jishu*, also a Feluda adventure. I was not aware of the global span that Feluda had captured. I also discovered that Feluda is visible and audible in present digital platforms. The question that arose in my mind was—how and why can an imaginary character have such wide acceptance across generations and over time. This quest for Feluda had motivated me to jump into this documentary.[2]

The documentary is roughly divided into two halves. The first half is filled with talking heads of directors, great fans spanning two generations of families, fans from abroad, scholars on Feluda and even one important author who has written an entire book on the character Jatayu who is a writer of popular detective thrillers himself but backed by no research at all. He becomes very fond of Feluda though the latter forever pokes him for his lack of knowledge. The second half is devoted to the films made on Feluda adventures both by Satyajit Ray and his son Sandip. This sequence drags after a point of time and needed some sharp editing to cut down on the footage.

Says Chatterjee:

> The written language, the nature of the crime, humour and characters are very modern. Any young adult today can easily relate to these factors. Another important factor is the childlike naivete that makes the characters and events very lovable for readers of all ages.

Through Feluda, Ray placed a common man in a tough crisis and helped him overcome the crisis. It is all about the triumph of the normal, regular man of the street grounded to his roots. The other characters such as Topshe, Jatayu, the writer of detective novels with intriguing titles, Sidhu Jetha, an old scholar Feluda often falls back on when he thinks Jetha will know the answer and their relationship with Feluda are also interesting. It would not be wrong to deduce that perhaps Ray introduced the concept of the global citizen.

An anecdote from Andrew Robinson's *Satyajit Ray: The*

Inner Eye perhaps best illustrates the popularity of the well-spun mystery. While shooting in Varanasi for the Feluda film, Joi Baba Felunath, Satyajit Ray had to contend with a problem. Overnight, a man from the local Bengali shop, Rinku Silk House plastered the location with posters of his shop, wanting to advertise his shop in a film that went on to become tremendously popular. Next day, the man turned up to enjoy the shoot too.

Feluda smoked filter-less Charminar cigarettes yet also practised yoga, was clean-shaven and nattily dressed. He could disarm the enemy with the perfect karate kick or whip out his Colt.32 snub-nosed pistol, but chose to use his '*mogoj*-astro' (brainpower) more often.

Soumitra Chatterjee, the first Feluda in the three films Ray made, says that he became a cult figure overnight after the first one *Sonal Kella* was released. 'Everyone I met on my morning walks began to address me as "Feluda", which was a surprise because I was already an established actor when *Sonar Kella* was released.' Ray's recorded voice interjects from time to time and this enriches the unfolding of the 'story'.

Says Sagnik Chatterjee:

> Documentaries and even fictional biopics are made on writers, painters, musicians and so on but this is a film which devotes one hour and 52 minutes on a fictional literary character that does not exist but is very real to those who have know him through his adventures and interesting ways of solving crimes. This has been a wonderful learning experience because

> during research and shooting, I met very important people from different fields who have been associated with Ray or his Feluda in different ways. I met and spoke to Soumitra Chatterjee who portrayed the first Feluda, then Sabyasachi Chakraborty, the next Feluda. But what excited me was my meeting with Ashis Nandy who analysed Feluda from a completely different perspective, investing the character with the quality of cosmopolitanism devoid of glamour and more stressed on values and human intellect.[3, 4]

'Feluda was what Bengalis aspired to be: brilliant, erudite, physically fit and mentally agile,' Deep Halder writes in *Daily O*. 'A perfect counter to his side-kick Lalmohan Babu, the balding, plump, nonsense-speaking, author of best-selling detective novels. Well-meaning, but a comic relief to Feluda's electrifying presence. Feluda was perfect. He could even smoke countless cigarettes and be fit with yoga and karate!'[5]

After Feluda's adventures were published in slim, hardcover novels, reached readers in Nepal and even Egypt.

Halder adds:

> Titled *Feluda Pherot (*The Return of Feluda) Srijit Mukherjee has two stories—*Chhinomostar Obhishaap and Jawto Kando Kathmandute*. And critics are divided. Do we love this Feluda (played by actor Tota Roy Chowdhury) or trash him? Do we let Feluda die with Soumitra Chatterjee or welcome a new one?

'Ray even built in Kolkata's severe outage phase in the 1970s and 1980s, when the city saw disruption in the electricity supply for 8-12 hours every day in *Mystery at Golok Lodge.*' The burglar uses the cover of darkness—predicted by the daily load-shedding schedule printed in newspapers—to escape,' notes Anuradha Sengupta in 'Watching the Detectives', an article in the magazine *Himal South Asia.*[6]

Atanu Ghosh, a noted director, points out how logical Ray was in placing his stories in a definite timeframe. Parapsychology, the science of remembering one's previous birth, was finally proved to be a 'science' in 1969 and Ray made *Sonar Kella* on the theme in 1970. Ray was particular about providing an authentic backdrop to his surreal story. The same applies to all the Feluda novels. Sunit Sengupta has written an entire book on Jatayu, the pen name of Lalmohan Ganguly, under the title *Jatayu Jindabad* (Laalmati, 2009). This character in the series is a popular writer of crime novels whose writing is never backed by research or authenticity. Though Feluda keeps poking him for his ignorance, over time, he becomes an ardent fan of Feluda and goes along with him wherever he travels. There is another senior character, Sidhu Jetha, an uncle of Feluda, who has every fact on his fingertips despite his age. The film details the character to complete the Feluda story.

Sandip Ray recounts in *Ami ar Feluda* how in 1970, when Feluda was just four stories old and had only appeared on the pages of *Sandesh* to the evident delight of its readers, Ray was accosted by the editor of the Bengali literary magazine *Desh.* He persuaded Ray to submit a Feluda novella for the annual autumnal issue. Not long after, Ray realised that the slot for a detective novel in that annual issue had been rendered vacant because of the death of Saradindu Bandopadhyay. So the same publication and same slot in which Byomkesh had regaled his readers for years and had to be retired, Feluda's breakthrough novel appeared. During Feluda's first adventure in the 1967 outing *Badshahi Angti* (The Emperor's Ring), he developed skills and habits that were going to be his hallmark throughout the series, right until the last big adventure *Gangtoke Gandogol* (Scandal in Gangtok). Topshe is seen growing up too, securing his place as the unopinionated narrator of his paternal cousin's thrilling adventures. Feluda's is a loveless and sexless universe full of a carefully calibrated, limited set of characters, a cyclical and identifiable pattern of clients and antagonists, set-piece thefts and murders, and a conscious—at times exasperating—determination not to overwhelm the self-imposed borders of permissibility in adolescent fiction.[7]

Chowdhury goes on to add that through the agency of the sleuth, Ray takes a severe stand against lost or wayward childhood. Many of the purveyors of crime are after all victims of bad upbringing, absent childhood, or difficult father-son relationships. Feluda's intervention is hence not just professional but ecumenical, a moral imperative to find closure to family fissures and restore order to a naturally edifying *bhadralok* familial order that reinforces the dominant sign of family hegemony. It would be a sweeping generalisation to claim that there are no women in Feluda's life. It is not so much about enumerating women in the stories as it is about the politics of configuring them in a certain way. There seems to be a customary, almost dogged insistence on a world underpopulated by women as long as that world belongs to children and young boys. This question has troubled commentators, but the analysis hardly goes beyond a customary complaint of their absence. Ray was not unaware of this tendency but seemed somewhat helpless to bring any closure to his own construction of a world without the female subject.

RAY'S CELLULOID CHILDREN

'Child is the father of man,' wrote Wordsworth in his poem, *My Heart Leaps Up* many years ago. But in the sphere of cinema, children are a species that has been systematically ignored. Because, so far as mainstream cinema goes, in Hindi films as well as regional language films, there are no children at all—they are all adults in miniature. Why? Why have directors present children as precocious kids mouthing adult homilies directed at adults, making value judgements on the behaviour of their parents, teachers and friends? Why must little boys and girls, from the days of *Anmol Ghadi*, *Deedar* and *Awara* through *Gunga Jumna* and *Kabhie Khushi Kabhie Ghum* exchange adult glances and fall in love much before they learn the meaning of the word? Why must that sweet little girl in *Kuchh Kuchh Hota Hai* not behave according to her age and keep harping on her father getting married to Anjali? Why?

These are rhetorical questions that have answers structured into them. Mainstream filmmakers treat child characters like appendages to the main characters or as a prologue to what is going to happen when the children grow up. Children are rarely permitted to act out their natural selves on screen. At a point of time, the characters they enact tend to rub off onto their personal lives and lifestyles and they grow into precocious, ill-mannered teenagers, utterly spoilt by parents, producers, directors and the acting and technical team. They rarely, if ever, grow up to become successful actors or stars as adults—

the only dream they nurtured as child actors.

But there are exceptions. Directors who have revealed a rare insight into the psyche of the child, who have been able to portray the innocence and naivete of the child, have been few and far between but not totally absent. Among them, those who shine like bright stars in a rather cloudy sky are Satyen Bose, Satyajit Ray, Ritwik Ghatak, Tapan Sinha, Gulzar, Shekhar Kapoor and Mani Ratnam. It may perhaps be wrong to leave out Kidar Sharma whose film for children *Jaldeep*, bagged the first ever international award in the history of children's cinema in India. But his child characters too, did not really perform like children do, and at times portrayed adults in miniature.

Utpalendu Chakraborty, a director who won acclaim with films like *Chokh* and *Debshishu*, made an interesting 77-minute documentary entitled *Child Artistes and Satyajit Ray.* Produced by Satarupa Sanyal under the banner of Human Art Centre, the film was granted the Censor Board's certification in 1997 but never released. This writer had the good fortune of having watched its only screening at Gorky Sadan, Kolkata, under the

auspices of The Eisenstein Cine Club a few years ago.

This is the only film in India to have explored the mastery of a filmmaker over children and his ability to handle them in such a way so as to make them appear as if they have been picked out of real life. The filmmaker is Satyajit Ray. From *Pather Panchali* to *Agantuk*, Ray tackled children as children. Yet, he took them out of their urban, educated, modern backdrop to place them in a rural setting as and when the script demanded. And not once did they appear out of place. Nor did they once behave or speak like adults.

Just close your eyes and think of Apu and Durga running through the *kaash* fields in *Pather Panchali* to see the train; a slightly grown-up Apu in *Aparajito* giving an oil massage to his mother's employer; the little Kajol asking his father whether he is a friend in *Apur Sansar*; the proud little orphan girl Ratan who refuses the one-rupee tip from her master in *Postmaster*; the exquisitely beautiful and tomboyish Mrinmoyee in *Samapti*; the child and teenage protagonists in the Feluda series of mystery films; the innocent little boy who asks his mother how to use white for a flower in a painting about his garden in *Pikoo*; the naïve grandson who asks his ailing grandfather what '*do numberi* money' means in *Shakha Proshakha*; and last, but never the least, the quiet little docile boy of *Agantuk* who is the only member of the family to place complete faith in the stranger who has arrived from nowhere. These are children created and nurtured by Ray through the magic of his imagination, his aesthetics and his humane sensibilities. They are children who transcend the synthetic boundaries of celluloid and the framed confines of the screen to step into our hearts and remain there forever.

Several boys were auditioned for the role of Apu but Ray was not satisfied with the results. His wife Bijoya spotted child actor Subir Banerjee playing on the neighbour's terrace and suggested his name to her husband. Now a middle-aged man, Subir Banerjee happily goes back to his memories of having worked in one of the best films in the world to have ever been made. 'I was too small to understand what was going on. But the director treated us as if we were all grown-up like him and made us feel relaxed and comfortable,' he says, adding, 'My father was not too keen to allow his son to act in a film. But Ray told him, "Today, no one knows your son or me. But I'll make a film that will change Bengali cinema. Then, all of Bengal will know both of us."' As author Bibhuti Bhushan Bandyopadhyay had passed away long before the inception of the film, Satyajit Ray had to get permission to make the film from his widow.

Like Uma Dasgupta, who played Durga, Subir did not appear in another film and worked modestly as a mill hand. Dasgupta, mother of two grown children, remembers the day when an assistant of the production unit met her in her school and asked her to play Durga because she resembled Karuna Banerjee, who played Sarbajaya. In a sequence, Durga steals a gold trinket from a neighbour's house, the neighbour insults Sarbajaya and she beats her daughter mercilessly till the little girl is half-dead. 'I've the most vivid memory of Karuna Banerjee beating me black and blue, and Ray exhorting her from the other end of the camera to deal still more naturalistic blows,' giggles Uma. She adds that there was no written script and shots were invented and prepared directly on the studio set. 'It made no difference to me and Subir as we had never faced a movie camera before and never faced one after. *Pather Panchali* was the only feature we acted in and I have no regrets,' sums up Uma.

Soumendu Roy who assisted cinematographer Subrata Mitra for *Pather Panchali* says:

> Satyajit Ray could study children's behaviour so flawlessly, you know…he could become their friend very easily and thus bring out the best in them. You must have noticed how the boy was calling out to Durga whom he had lost sight of; he moved a few steps ahead and then stopped for a short while, jumped over some ditches; looked around the field and then continued his search for his sister for the scene of their roaming across the field before they caught sight of the train. Only Ray could achieve this.

There are others such as the little girl Ratan in *Postmaster*, who refuses the tip the postmaster gives her, turns away without speaking to him and as the camera shows her face, we see tears trickling down. Mrinmoyee in *Samapti* is a girl-bride who refuses to take her bride identity seriously and continues her naughty pranks, much to the concern of her kindly mother-in-law and surprised husband. She runs away in the middle of the night on her nuptial night to feed her pet squirrel!

Talking about his experience of having worked with Ray, Kushal Chakravorty who played the main role in Ray's *Sonar Kella* and is now a well-known television hero, laughingly says that at that time, he was too little to understand who Ray was and why he was considered such a larger-than-life personality. Nor was he one to make his child actors conscious of the fact that they were acting. Kushal recalls:

> His gift lay in that that he never treated us like children. I would play chess with him between shoots and I would win every time. Maybe, he allowed me to win. I would be surprised to find my father in constant awe of him. This treatment of placing children on an equal platform helped us open up. All we had to do was to act ourselves, to be natural. In the given ambience, as far as I can remember, I don't think it was difficult. Come to think of it, it was quite easy. Really.

Siddhartha Chatterjee, who played the teenaged Topshe, assistant to his uncle, the self-styled detective Feluda, maintained a diary when he acted in the two Feluda films directed by Ray. When Ray shot *Sonal Kella (The Golden Fortress)*, Chatterjee was still in school. When Ray shot *Joy Baba Felunath* in 1977, the schoolboy was doing in the second year of his Bachelor of Commerce degree and his articleship for his Chartered Accountancy exams at the same time. Pages from his diary reveal a few facets of Ray not only as a director par excellence but also as a person who could shape the character of the people he worked with.

According to Chatterjee, though naughty at home, he shied away from people outside.

> I got rid of my shyness over the shooting of Sonar Kella in Rajasthan. In fact, you could now call me an extrovert. The three facets of Ray's persona I found to be the most fascinating are (a) his total control over any situation related directly or indirectly to his work, (b) his ability to take speedy and instantaneous decisions and (c) time management. In fact, my Topshe character has carried over to my daughter's school. When she bagged the first prize at the fancy dress contest, her teachers asked her where she had honed her acting skills from. Her prompt response was, "Why, from my father of course. Don't you know that he is the Topshe from all the Feluda films?" But I don't act anymore. That is the impact of Ray and his Feluda.

The little Kaajal, Apu's son, who, ill-treated by his maternal grandfather, asks his father if he is a 'friend' and Apu says 'Yes, I am your friend,' picks the little boy up, perches him on his shoulders and sets out to travel across the world.

Some outstandingly brilliant characterisations and portrayals of the child on celluloid away from Satyajit Ray films deserve mention alongside his celluloid children. These are the two boys in Satyen Bose's biggest commercial hit *Jagriti*, the runaway boy in Ritwik Ghatak's *Bari Thekey Paliye*, the podgy little Minu (the late Tinku Tagore) who fails to recognise her Kabuliwalla friend when she grows up in Tapan Sinha's

Kabuliwalla, the two boys in Gulzar's classic film *Kitaab*, the three memorable kids in Shekhar Kapoor's *Masoom*, the small boy who breaks into tears when he runs the wrong way in Ashutosh Gowarikar's *Lagaan*, and the lovable little kids in Mani Ratnam's *Anjali*.

At the end of it all, we are reminded of Pablo Picasso who said, 'Every child is an artist. The problem is how to remain an artist once we grow up.' Only three among these children grew up to become actors. One of them is Kushal Chakravorty, who played the central character in Ray's *Sonar Kella* in 1972. The second one is Jaya Bachchan who, as Jaya Bhaduri, played the role of Arati's impish, childish, schoolgoing sister-in-law in Ray's *Mahanagar*. The third is Aparna Sen who made her debut as the tomboyish teenage bride, Mrinmoyee in *Samapti*.

THE CONTROVERSY OVER COLOURISATION

More than a decade ago, the film page editor of a Kolkata daily asked me to do a comparative review of *Mughal-e-Azam* in black-and-white and the remake in colour because he could not find any journalist he knew who had watched both versions. I was delighted and since the colour version was quite fresh in my mind, sat down to do the review. To me, a lavishly mounted historical romance with a glamorous star cast looked better than the original. But the print was much less than perfect so I awarded more marks, mentally, to the original where the visuals were very clear. Other than that, I did not think that there was much qualitative difference between the two versions if the audience were taken into account.

Now comes the news that a 2.14-minute video of Satyajit Ray's classic *Pather Panchali* has been converted through AI (Artificial Intelligence) into colour. The experiment has been done by Aniket Bera, 30, professor at the University of Maryland, near Washington DC. He did it while in quarantine during the COVID-19 outbreak and uploaded it on 14 May, initiating a heated debate on whether a world classic should be touched upon even through AI. Of course, the very young Bera insists that he did it as an experiment.

The issue at stake is two-fold: whether colour should at all be attempted on a classic film or whether this can be applied to other films per se. I have not watched this small slice of video yet but those who have, express widely divergent opinions.

Before come to the nitty-gritty of this debate, let us trace our steps backwards in time.

According to a well-researched study on this subject, film scholar and author Amitava Nag wrote in 'The Colour of Aesthetics' in *Silhouette,* an online magazine he edits:[9]

> A Mumbai-based firm, Sankranti Creations (which added colour to *Mughal-e-Azam* and *Naya Daur*) has proposed to the West Bengal government that owns the Ray classic to colour the movie. The company has set a budget of over Rs 1 crore for the colour project (for a team of 70) and a plan to release it by the end of 2008. However, there are more controversies in store—Sankranti Creations claims it has already converted one minute of *Pather Panchali* into colour and sent the demo clip along with its proposal to the West Bengal government. However, the concerned government officials deny any knowledge of such a proposal. Amidst this confusion, most of the intelligentsia—the film-makers, journalists, critics and others, all feel shocked and took little time to hit back.

> *Mughal-e-Azam* and *Naya Daur* were manually coloured frame by frame, which cost a lot of money. Using the AI technology, this entire process can be automated and done for free because the technology is open sourced! Use of technology is better than manual work in this case. In the YouTube video, one can see the difference between the older and latest version. It's not just colour but a big quality improvement.
>
> I am quite intrigued to look at the negotiations that take place through Artificial Intelligence. But I would not want to watch *Pather Panchali* in colour. The entire creativity of the original will raise questions springing from the fact that every technician from the cinematographer to the editor, art director and costume designer at the time the film was made, had a definite concept in mind which was specific to and limited by the technology available at the time the film was made. How can the colourisation recreate those aesthetics, artistry and skill involved?

This was a sharp comment from the noted Bengali filmmaker Atanu Ghosh who has won a National Award for one of his films.

According to Amitava Nag, 'A Kolkata-based TV Channel, *24 Ghanta* conducted an SMS survey on 28 March 2008 where a whopping 96 per cent responded that *Pather Panchali* needed no colour to uplift its quality or appeal to contemporary viewers. If we look into Hollywood, the conflict over colourising of black-white films started back in the 1980s,' writes Nag going on to add: 'Ted Turner was a pioneer in conceptualising this—he hired American Film Technologies to colourise hundreds of films acquired from MGM in 1986. Inadequate technology (though at every point in time any technology that is twenty years old seems inadequate!) resulted in unreal tones and left much to be desired.'

Coming back to the present controversy, some filmmakers and viewers have gone gaga over the brilliant quality of the visual images while most others are aghast at the tampering of a world-class classic. One also has to remember the ambience of a Bengal village created to represent the literary ambience created by Bibhuti Bhushan Bandopadhyay on whose novel the film was made. However, Ray himself was roundly criticised for using colour for *Ashani Sanket* also based on a Bandopadhyay classic of the same name set against the backdrop of the Bengal famine. But Ray hit back at his critics by stating that ideas and beliefs held by the general audience about the use of colour in cinema are inextricably linked with glamour, which also implies that the painful existence of people in the lower strata of society cannot be successfully portrayed through colour. This, indeed, was the general consensus till a few years before *Ashani Sanket* was made—that a serious subject and colour did not go together. He reasoned that such a view is more predominant in India where commercial profitability shapes aesthetic taste more than anywhere else.

But this writer can offer another logic about why Ray made this film in colour. The 1943 Bengal famine was historically established to have been a man-made one and not due to any crop failure or natural calamity. Perhaps colour was used to reaffirm that everything was right with Nature and yet people were starving to death. Colour would establish the contrast between the machinations of the British then and how these impacted on the village people in Bengal which took a toll of around two million lives out of the then total population of sixty million in Bengal province.

In the present scenario, one of the most vocal attacks comes from Prof Madhuja Mukherjee, who teaches Film Studies at Jadavpur University and is also a filmmaker in her own right. According to Mukherjee:

> Colourisation of *Pather Panchali* does a great disservice to the cinematographer of the film, Subrata Mitra. All tonalities, the grey tones or what Mitra described as *sargam* have been erased...all light intensity are same, skin tones are similar, walls merge with characters—because they are all brown—the density of the image and the long shots have been destroyed as though it was washed with chlorine. It's frankly a very very sloppy work with no understanding of history of colour and technology in cinema.
>
> If Mitra had disowned *Devi* after he saw it on TV (because of the high contrast restoration) I am wondering what he would have done now…It is like me trying to do something with Monalisa because so many others did it. Indeed, I have been thinking for some time now that quarantine has affected our brains

> in really adverse ways. The other thing that concerns me deeply are the types of colours used both for saris and for the skin tones. I am not sure if it works as an App or not but in another case—colourisation of the song *'Jane kya tune kahi'* from the film *Pyaasa*—I saw the same mauve tones for Waheeda Rahman's sari! Also the skins are more or less the same! I am wondering if there are some plugins for 'Indian skin tones'. I am sorry but we are perhaps fifty shades of brown! As said before, above all it's really poorly done, very unthoughtful.

Filmmaker Judhajit Sarkar, a FTII alumnus, says:

> American tycoon Ted Turner took over a number of bankrupt Hollywood production companies. He had his own channel TMC which showed these (horribly) colourised films. There was mixed reaction but the makers who were still alive vehemently protested. A petition was also sent to the President. Martin Scorsese was one of the vocal leaders. Satyajit Ray

being a sensible and sensitive artist would never have supported such a blasphemous act.

Amartya Bhattacharya, whose film is winning prizes across the globe, presents a different point of view:

> 'Black and white is not the unavailability of colour, it is a different aesthetic altogether. Yes, in those times, there were no colours, and that was a restriction so films were conceived in black and white. It is not just the output that is black and white. It is an assembly of too many things that together creates a synergy. The synergy makes or breaks a film. Films or photographs are never the same if the same compositions are coloured.' With colour, the entire aesthetic changes. The compositions would change, the use of lights would change, the use of shadows would change, even the edit could change at times. It's never the same. I know cinema is just a commodity to most people, but it's better to remember a film the way it was conceived. And no, I don't have any Ray hangover or obsessions whatsoever. Emotions don't move me. It's just an unbiased objective view. I am 100 per cent in support of experiment; of whatever kind it is. But behind every experiment there has to be a strong reasoning and a deep perception of the substrate on which the experiment is been carried out.

Filmmaker Nirmal Chakravarty makes a very interesting comment.

> Rituparno Ghosh made his film *Dosar* in black and white. If someone were to decide to turn it into colour, imagine what the film would look like. Of course, it would be a different matter if someone would write a completely new script of the same story and make a completely different *Pather Panchali* in colour.

Sudeshna Ghosh, a journalist, raises a pertinent question:

> I can understand people doing experiments in quarantine, but I am totally against the idea of implementing the same on classics. Colour and tone of a film are integral in conveying the mood and story that a filmmaker intended to convey. Changing that changes the aesthetics of the film. I cringe at the thought of the iconic train scene with the *Kashphool* in colour! And we had our first colour film in 1932. Even if it was not popular till late '50s, don't you think a meticulous man and perfectionist like Ray would have made it in colour if he thought that was the best way to tell his story?

Shubhrajit Mitra, a noted filmmaker, says:

> Though the effort is praiseworthy, the tonal quality lacks richness and emotional depth. It looks like an average below grade film of the 1960s visually. It was originally shot keeping the black and white, grey scale aesthetics in mind. Eastman Kodak colour negative of the 50s/60s look was different. Sarbajaya is wearing a blue saree instead of red bordered Bengali cotton, which

> should have been the original colour. There are other glaring flaws such as the lack of reproducing the rural skin tone which shows lack of research on the part of the creator. Colour is the most essential part of a visual to convey the mood. *Pather Panchali* is meant for black and white. The subject demanded colour—at least in the one we are discussing.

Turqaaz Firozi, an award-winning documentary filmmaker who is part of the faculty at the SRFTII in Kolkata, is surprised at the hue and cry this debate over the colouring of *Pather Panchali* has created.

> What's the big hue and cry about the colouring of a few frames or sections of *Pather Panchali* with AI or otherwise? As an academic experiment or otherwise? Nobody can change the original, it remains in its pristine form, we cannot undo its impact, so what's wrong? Let us not make a sacred cow out of a film masterpiece. Let it be viewed, played around with, knocked down, done over, remixed, celebrated, ridiculed, whatever—why not? The elitist sacred versus profane debate this has set up is truly surprising.

Think of Federico Fellini's *8½* in colour, or Eisenstein's *Battleship Potemkin* or Ingmar Bergman's *Wild Strawberies* in colour. You get the picture in black and white. Let the debate rest on this quizzical note, for now.

Endnotes

1 *Professor Shanku*, Satyajit Ray, Newscript, 1965.

2. *Feludar Goendagiri* (Felu-da's detecting skills), Satyajit Ray in Bengali magazine, *Sandesh*,1965.

3. From an interview with the late Badal Bose who said this was one of the biggest blockbusters in the Bengali publishing industry and he was proud that Ababda Publishers had published these books.

4. *Satyajit Ray: The Inner Eye*, Andrew Robinson, University of California Press, 1 Nov 1989.

5. *Feluda is Dead: A New Feluda is Born, Long Live Feluda* Deep Halder in *Daily O* 5 Jan 2021.

6. *Watching the Detectives*, Anuradha Sengupta, Himal South Asian, 8 Nov 2013.

7. *Jatayu Jindabad*, Sunit Sengupta, Laalmati, 2009.

HANDWRITTEN LETTERS BY SATYAJIT RAY TO THE AUTHOR

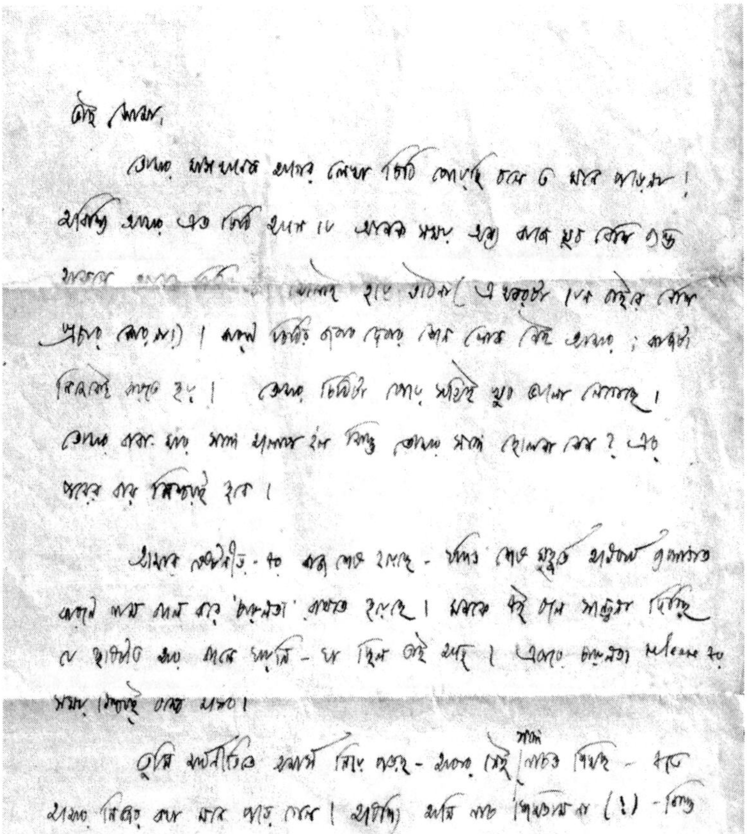

Satyajit Ray's letter dated 28.03.64 (Page one)

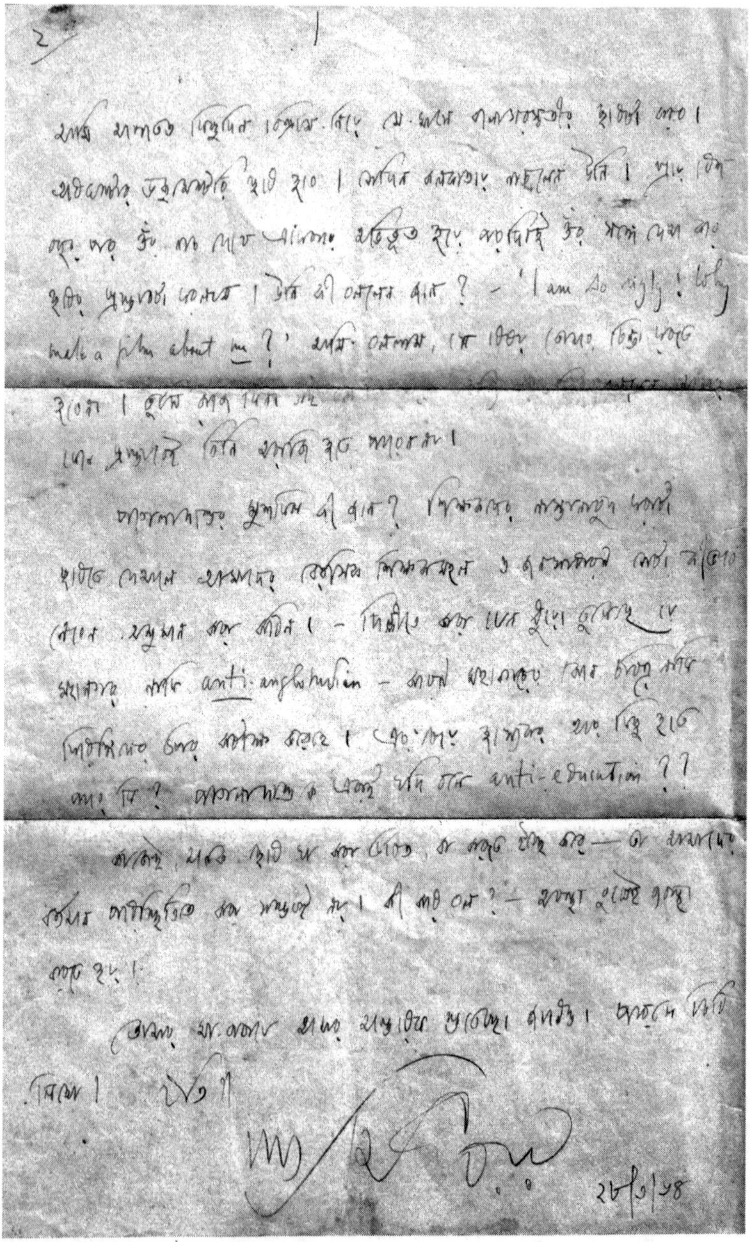

Satyajit Ray's letter dated 28.03.64 (Page two)

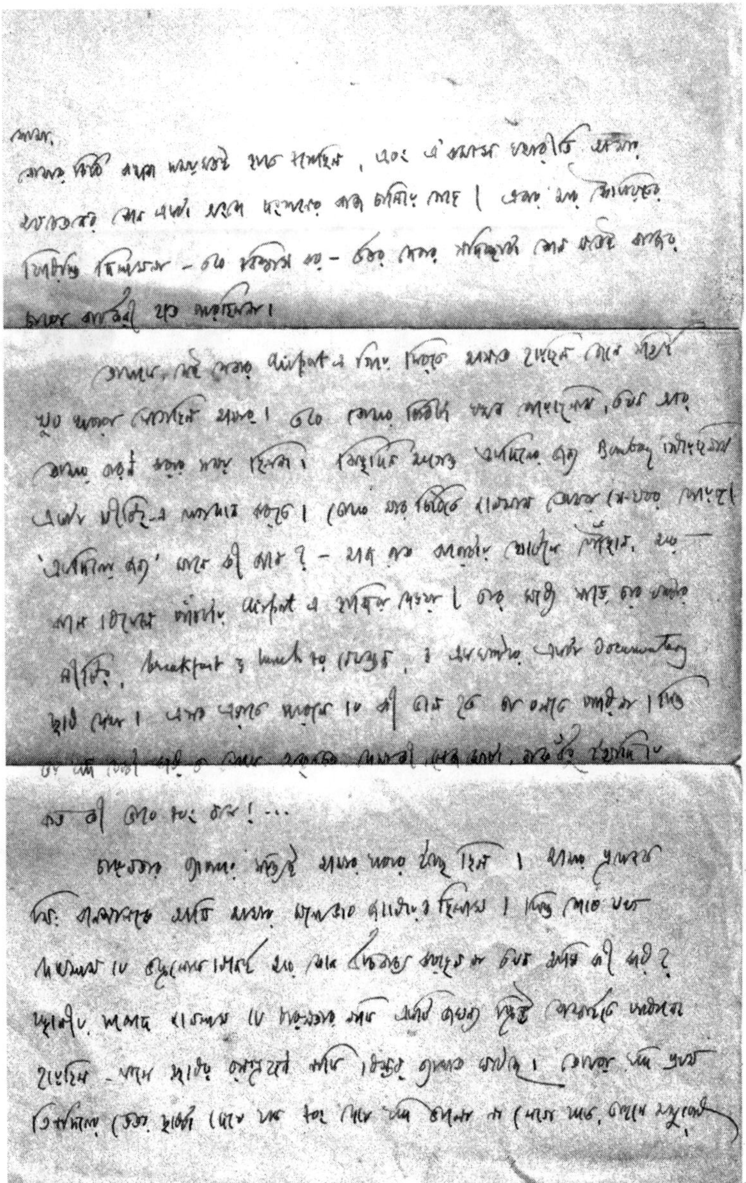

Satyajit Ray's letter dated 1.6.64 (Page one)

Satyajit Ray's letter dated 1.6.64

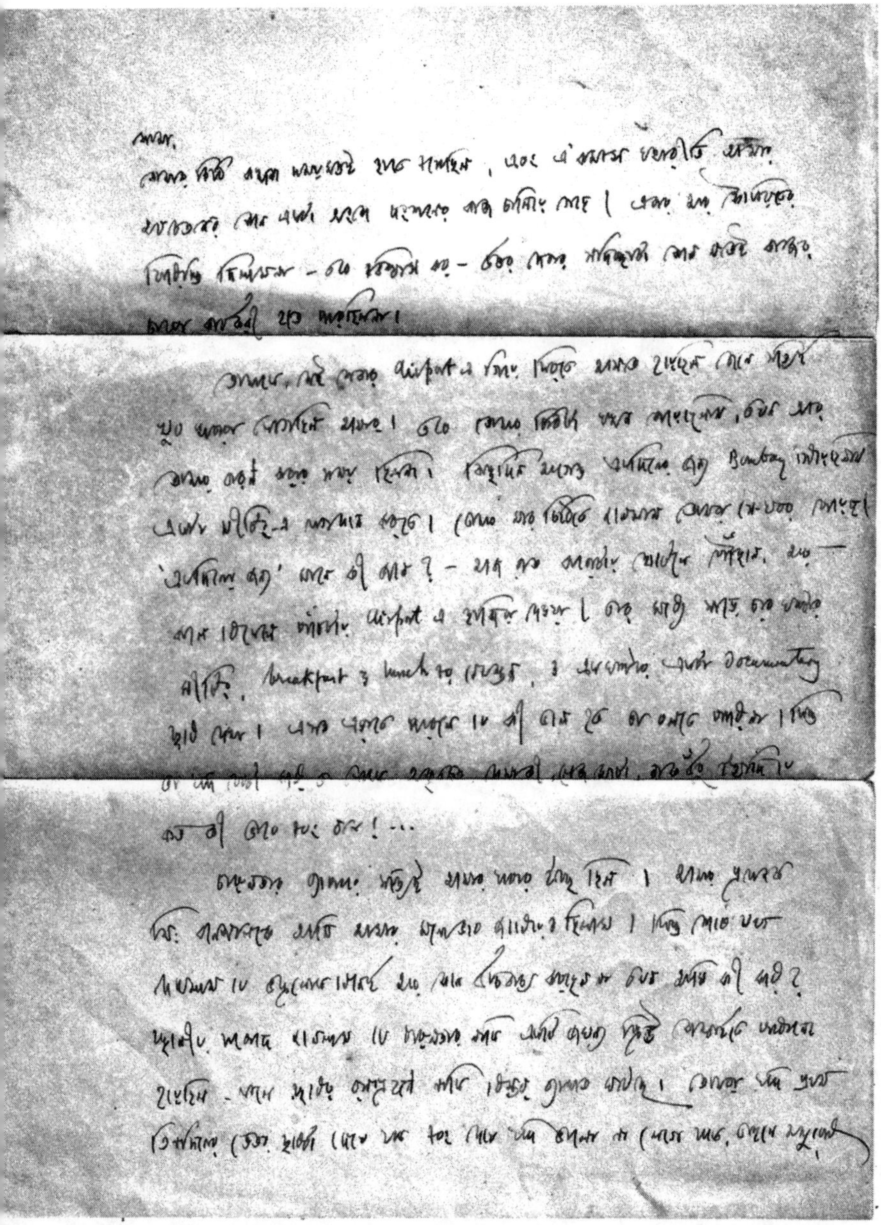

Satyajit Ray's letter dated 9.9.64 (Page one)

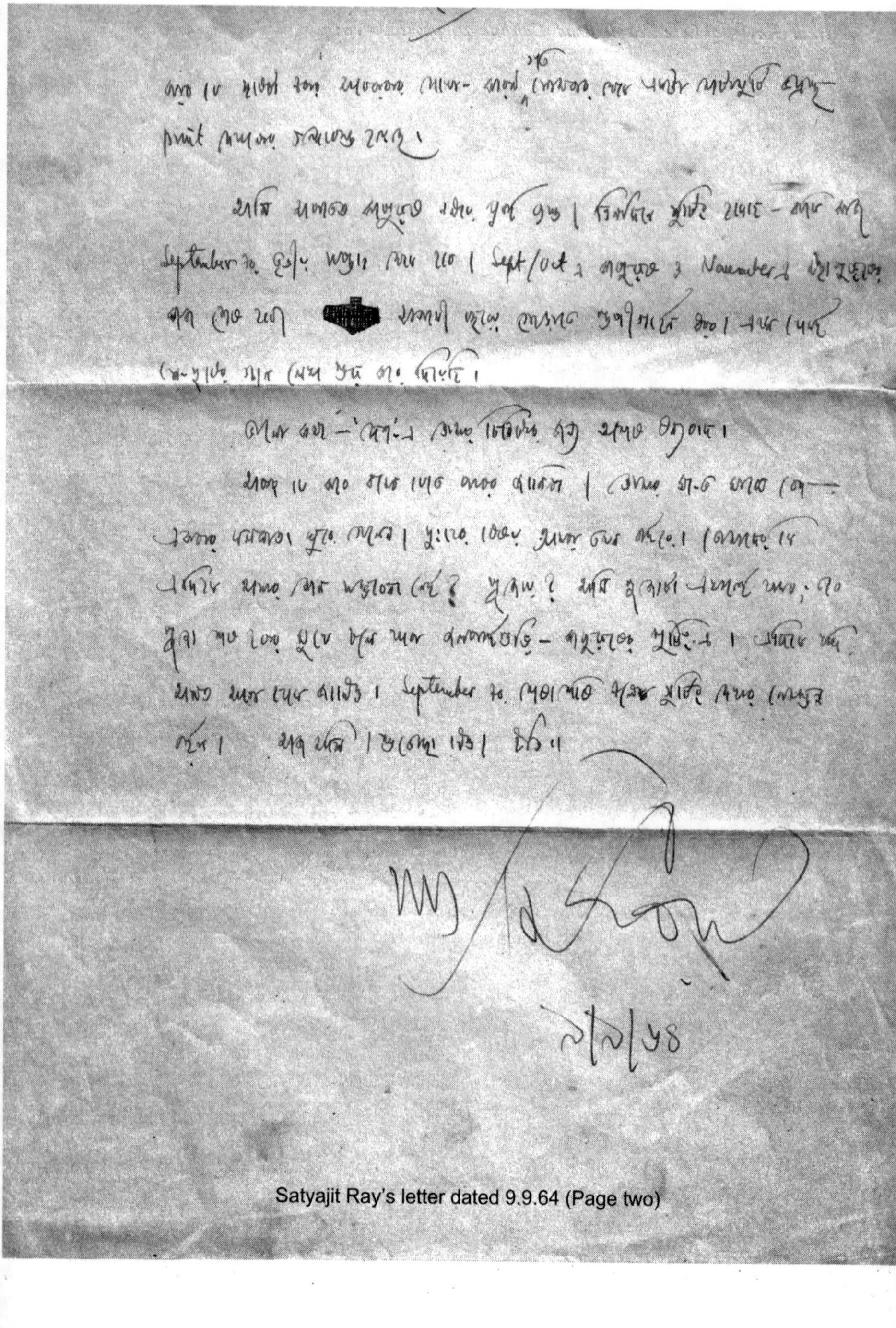

Satyajit Ray's letter dated 9.9.64 (Page two)

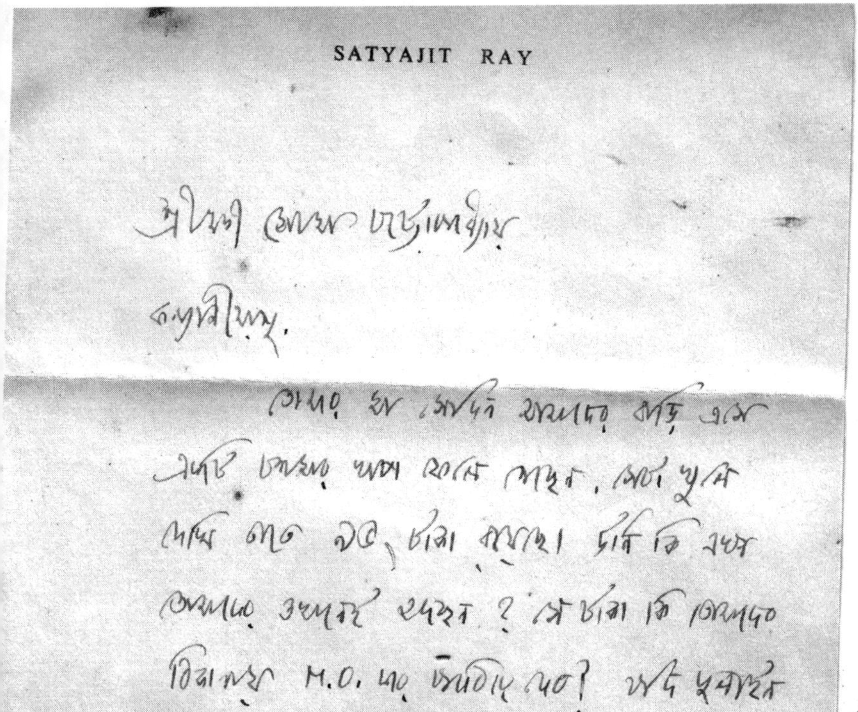

SATYAJIT RAY

শ্রীমতী সোমা চট্টোপাধ্যায়

কল্যাণীয়াসু,

তোমরা যে সেদিন আমাদের বাড়ি এসে একটি টাকার খাম ফেলে গেছেন, সেটা খুলে দেখি তাতে ৩০, টাকা রয়েছে। টাকা কি এখন আমাদের এখানেই থাকবে? না টাকা কি তোমাদের ঠিকানায় M.O. করে পাঠিয়ে দেব? যদি দু-লাইন লিখে জানাও তো খুব ভাল হয়।

তোমার লেখা চিঠির এখানে-সেখানে ভুল, তবে লেখা ভাল। আশা করি ভাল আছ। ভাল থেকো।

শুভেচ্ছান্তে

সত্যজিৎ রায়

২৪।১।৮৪

Satyajit Ray’s letter dated 24.1.84 on his letter head